7/17/99 _Joel Randall_

Reflections

&

Perceptions

From the Land of
Grass & Buffalo

Joel Randall

English Usage
Reflections & *Perceptions*

English is one of the most difficult languages in the world to learn, primarily due to complicated rules and the frequent exceptions to 'em. What you have to do is memorize the hole (whole) deal.

English teachers and most folks go along with attorneys and governments (societies?) efforts to make things more complicated, there appears a need to make English and life simpler. Looks like progress will have to come from grass roots folks like us livin in grass country.

My spellin through as thru and night as nite are examples of my contribution.

Words that are spelled different than Websters are meant to be pronounced as spelled. A common occurrence in **Refections &** *Perceptions* is the dropping of the g on ing.

Warning: I'm not consistent

Refections & *Perceptions* contains Soul Food.

WELCOME...

...to my book of stories and poems.

You are in this book!

Your roots & cultures,

Your thoughts & questions,

Your fears & taboos,

Your pleasures & pains.

THANKS

Thank you readers.

Thanks to all who helped with this book.

Thanks to my family, Grey Antelope,

friends and lovers.

Published by
Heartland Publishing
P.O. Box 1721
Kearney, NE 68848
1-308-468-5266

ISBN 0-9661865-1-6

Printed by
Morris Press
Kearney, Nebraska

Photos by
Mary Wales North
Lexington, Nebraska

Typesetting and Design by
Chris Eggleston
Pleasanton, Nebraska

BATHROOM BLESSING

Bathrooms take up a lot of peoples' time. Hunting bathrooms, building bathrooms, remodeling bathrooms, supplying bathrooms, cleaning bathrooms, and repairing bathrooms. Not to mention #1 & #2, washing & primping oneself to socially interact as a presentable person after leaving the bathroom.

Higher forms of life (this being animals & birds), being more natural and sane, are able to go to the bathroom while doing their normal activities, without all the fuss. Birds have evolved to the highest state, combining the two bathroom functions into one. They have developed the skill of going to the bathroom, even while flying.

The more time you spend out in nature, the better chance you have of being blessed.

I CAN REMEMBER

I can remember when the backyard barbecue first became popular. We were young, newly married. We had to have one. They were over priced, wobbly, light weight and junky. I made one from a small antique forge. Fabricated a grille, made a new leather belt and freed-up the fan. With some black spray paint, it was a Jim-dandy. Weighing close to 100#, guaranteed to last 400 years.

We invited my parents and grandparents over for the grand event. When the fire was right I added the steaks and went in for a drink of water. When I came out, surprise, the flames were 4 feet high and rising. I grabbed the garden hose and got everything under control. The fat had definitely caught on fire. I cooked the steaks some more. They were black on the outside and raw inside. We feasted on real barbecue at last, it was great, almost. We were sitting around the picnic table visiting and remembering the past after dessert when my grandfather said, "I can remember when people used to eat in the house and shit outside."

NO, WE WEREN'T POOR

Nice outhouse
painted white
window too.
No roll
catalog.

Went to town
every other
Saturday nite.
Visited on the corner
traded eggs
for groceries.
Sold the cream
for cash.

No, we weren't poor.

In the summertime
last stop
ice
big block.

In the fall
new shoes
for school.
Bought some
coal too.

No, we weren't poor.

COMMON SENSE

It ain't as common as it usta be.

ANOTHER ILLUSION

Another dollar will solve the problem.
Another government agency will solve
    the problem.
Another drug will solve the problem.
Another committee will solve
    the problem.
ANOTHER ILLUSION.
Another gadget will solve the problem.
Another law will solve the problem.
Another scientific discovery will solve
    the problem.
ANOTHER ILLUSION
Another weapon will solve the problem.
Another war will solve the problem.
ANOTHER ILLUSION.

THE BALANCE

When I was young, the old
    sat around and watched me work.
Now I'm old and the young
    sit around and watch me work.

ALL IS POSSIBLE

All is possible,
if you're willing
to do anything.
Even change.
Care ever
forever.
All is possible

ALL IS POSSIBLE

LOVE

Love changes everything
    and everything changes
She was in my thoughts
    She was in my dreams
She was in my days
    She was in my nites
And, all my troubles
    are, of my own making
And, cars have gotten smaller
    trucks have gotten bigger
Love changes everything
    and everything changes
      -- Even Love --
And sometimes
    Egos get bigger
      Hearts get smaller
And then
She was in my face
    Agendas getting bigger
    Voices getting louder
    Hearts getting smaller

SEX

The truth is seldom popular.
The truth is, sex is popular,
most anyone, can do it,
allright and there's some,
can do it all nite.
Practice doesn't make perfect,
but, sometimes it helps, along with,
proper attitude, and love to share.

Trouble is cheap, to get into to, but expensive to get out of.

BEEN

I've been good
I've been bad

I've been happy
I've been sad

I've been right
I've been wrong

and

You're gonna miss me
when I'm gone.

BITTERSWEET

Some what
Innocent.

I disappeared
into her
wild sweetness.

Not expecting
to learn
more of
life's lessons.

Some what
Bittersweet.

I have been trying to seize the promises
which they made me -- but I cannot find them.
Big Bear

COMMON SENSE

In the country when I was a boy everyone left the keys in their vehicles. No one ever locked a door, most doors didn't even have locks. If they did, no one knew where the keys were. In those days everyone knew everybody around. In an emergency you were expected to just go on in, make a phone call or borrow whatever you needed.

I remember hearing on the radio that Charlie Starkweather was in the area killing people and stealing cars. Roadblocks were being set up everywhere. The police were warning everyone to make sure they had taken the keys out of their cars.

Our neighbor walked out and got the car keys and laid them on the kitchen table. After eating he just sat there looking at the car keys for a long time. Then he picked them up and went out and put them back in the car. When he returned to the house he said "I sure wouldn't want anyone like that coming up to the house to get the keys."

THE BEAUTY OF SILENCE

Long time gone.
The great whales
singing could be
heard around the world.
Long time gone.
The beauty of silence.
Long since disappeared
into the noise of
progress.
The beauty of silence.
Long time gone.

DEEPER THAN THE OCEAN

Blue, green, some grey
always moving, always changing
some dancing, some prancing
always rising, always falling
some beauty, more energy
some magic, more mystery

Blue, green, some grey
reflecting love & life
disappearing into eternity
her eyes
deeper than the ocean

DEEPER MEANIN

Wrecked again
makin mistakes
makin changes
continued learnin
deeper meanin
Gettin slower
gettin older
makin changes
changin resentments
and anger

into gratitude and deeper meaning
More peace
more serenity
more gratitude
more learning

more lessons
Always coming
with deeper meaning

DEATH

Old enough to be deeply aware of death, watched & observed enough dyin & suffering to know that sometimes the greatest gift & blessing is death.

> Older now
> Deeply aware
> of Death
> No, I'm not afraid
> of Death
> I'm afraid
> of the pain & suffering
> before death
> No, I'm not afraid
> of Death.

HE SAID, I SAID

He said "It's really good to die for something you really believe in."

I said "that's kinda hard because the only thing I really believe in is living."

EGO

> How big is your ego?
> Big enough, to drown you
> in your own - shit.

> It is better to stand on the large boulder
> than to be under it.

ILLUSION OF HAPPINESS

When we were young
    wild and crazy
We did it all
    more or less
In the open

I had
    many friends
All equally prone
    to be
Wicked and evil

When I was young
    I was
        Happier than
A toad in Hell

Illusion of Happiness

THE KISS

New York City
crowded street
walkin along
I didn't see
Surprise
Wet kiss
people fear
people gaspin
people movin
Wet kiss
on the check

Pit Bull
disappearing

SICK

Are You
    so sick
that
    you think
I'm well?

Are you
    that sick?

TWO OBSERVATIONS

I observed
a straight man
catching hell
from a lesbian woman
for womanizing
and acting like
a male chauvinist pig

Later
I observed
a lesbian woman
same one
hitting on a woman
    womanizing
and acting like
a male chauvinist pig
    or should I say
A female chauvinist pig?

SECURITY

Security is one's inner relationship
with the Great Spirit

TRUTH

The loud voice
of anger
lost in itself.
The soft voice
of truth
found in love.
Partly heard
partly felt.
Seldom understood
Truth

HERE I AM

Once upon a time

I took the fast track
to hell and back
and that's a fact

Long ago
I jumped, from
the frying pan
into the fire

It was hotter
more alive

I jumped again
and
Here I am

I am opening my heart to speak to you ---
open yours to receive my words.
Como

WHY I'M STILL HERE

Death, not yet
    this fool tried
        came damn close
My friend Death
    pushed me back
        not yet, not yet
His lessons come high
    my friend, and
        there's easier ways
Death ain't talked about much in this
Culture. It's kinda funny, all the
things people do to hurry death along.

Good, bad, young, old, fat, skinny
healthy, sickly, beautiful, ugly,
short, tall, peaceful, violent,
Rich, poor, saintly, criminal.

Death Always near
    Good behavior
        no exceptions
I got a
    Karmic Extension
        Bad behavior
And that's, why I'm still here

NOSTALGIA

Nostalgia is one more
    thing that gets better
        with age

The more things change, the more they remain insane.

THE FUNERAL

Family dinner, mortuary
introductions, small talk
seating arranged
curtain opening, slowly
electric motor, struggling
serious expressions
for this time
place of death.

Preacher preaching
lies and more lies, dead mother
the American dream, mother fantasies
alive and well
bury the secrets
the pain, the denial.

Beautiful flowers
hairdressers, neighbors
family & friends.

9 year old sez, you ain't gonna
bury them pearls are you?
How much did, they cost?

Cemetery - graveside
raining & cold, only a few.
preacher, run down
short & sweet.

Leaving, 3 kernels, blue corn.
Red rose bud, on the ground, picked up.

Another Family dinner.

YOUNG

Old days
    old cars

Long days
    short nights
under the stars
    dreamin & schemin
short nights
    long days

old days
    old cars
laughin at
    the scars

Young

HOO DOO

Hoo Doo
    Hoo Doo
        Voodoo Too
Hoo Doo
    Hoo Doo
        Voodoo Too
Hoo Doo
    Hoo Doo
        You Love
Hoo Doo
        You Love
Hoo Doo
    Hoo Doo
        Voodoo Too

Get out of your own way.

WOUNDED HEART

Nebraska orphanages
foster homes.
Too young
too poor.
Father
like a turkey
in the corn
long gone.
Hung, KKK.
Too Indian
too crazy.
Stepfather
town joke.
Problems, poverty
junk.
A shack
ragged & cold.
Downtown
selling "Grit."
Older sisters
escaping
going wild.
Older brother
deformed, diseased.
incest -
Syphilis.
Wounded heart.
My mother
wounded heart.

SUPPORT

The police
armed
and dangerous

Support
your local
Poet.

VALUE OF COLLEGE WORK

She was real proud of the A she received on her 5000 word college paper and the quality of work that she had put into it. She described the class and her high esteem for both the class & the professor.

I asked her if she had kept the paper and she replied "what on earth for?"

WE WERE TEENAGERS

The nites were short
　　raising hell
The days were long
　　working hard
A short time ago
　　when
We were teenagers

We knew it all
　　Had all the answers
　　　　but
Them answers
　　slipped away
With the years
　　and
the mistakes

RELATIONSHIPS UNHAPPINESS

Relationships: 2 major causes of unhappiness
1. Because you're in a relationship.
2. Because you're not in a relationship.

The best things in life are not things.

SUICIDE

Basic freedom to come & go
believed in somewhat
don't apply to suicide.
Taking oneself on that one way trip
to where life goes
ain't socially acceptable.
The changes comes slow and hard,
and the heats on Dr. Kovarkian.
Accidents are socially acceptable
and many accidents are suicides denied
and they are easily overlooked.
Alcohol, tobacco & drugs
taxes paid in full
Socially acceptable suicide.

HELLO

Hello
Hell - o
o - Hell
Go to Hell
Hell - o
o - Hell
Hello

Time can heal, but, it don't pay the bills.

Guilty until proven wealthy.

SCARRED

Scars and muscles
scars and men.
Evidence
of violence
in life.
Men
in prison
lost children.
Criminals
caught
reenacting childhood
as adults.
Tough, macho
proving manhood
and false egos.
Scars and men
prison abuse.
Prison humor
shucking & jiving,
hiding the pain
insulating the past.
Scars and men
scars from
fathers, families
toughboys, men.
Unwanted gifts
from society.
Scars & wounds.
Scarred.

PAIN

I have labor pains
how strange
for I am a man.
Giving birth to myself
becoming a new man
I have labor pains.
Love lost, childhood missed
mourning, grieving the past
I have much pain.
Shamed & abused as a child
deep wounds, old wounds
years of denied pain.
Out of hiding, my inner child
complaining, crying & yelling
expressing the pain.
Addictions no longer working
escaping is not possible
reality, feeling the pain.
Growing, changing and feeling
letting go, being present
I have pain.
Reparenting my inner child
loving, nurturing & supporting
I have joy & pain.
Facing my fears, my illusions
learning about love, intimacy
I have hope.
Opening my heart
feeling my feelings
I am healing & recovering.
Grateful for the program
doing the inner work
welcoming the labor pains.

Crazy Horse didn't drink.

SPEAK

Speak your mind, Speak your heart. My children, speak. They are waiting, they are listening.

Speak to Father Sun, Mother Earth, the birds, the animals, the plants, the trees, the rocks, the water, the wind. They are all listening.

Speak, my children, speak, speak your mind, speak your heart.

LOVE AND PAIN

To love is sometimes painful, not to love is more painful.

BACKCOUNTY LAWS

Backcountry, way back
where laws of man
were not important
Backcountry, where actions
are more important
than words

BUMPER STICKER

Horn broken, watch for finger.

VULTURE RESPECT

Vultures respect all life, waiting patiently, with the gift of time, for death.

EXPERIENCE

I went alone
  to the River.
I was quiet
  nature came closer.
The vital message
  I am part of it.
I stayed longer
  the spirits came.
I faced my fears
  they were nothing
    when
The experience came
  beyond my fears.
I experienced & understood
  yet beyond understanding.
I deeply know
  I am more than human.
I am not afraid of life.
  The Vision Quest.

EARLY MEMORY

Small child
The farm.

Cold, winter
night.

Upstairs
heavy blankets
piled high.

Hot iron
wrapped
in a towel.

Warm feet.
Sleep.

Early morning
frost
on the covers.

DOT Dept. of Transportation

We can shut down any truck
any driver, any time, any place.

Greenhorn driver education plan.
Free, not quite, minimum fine
150 dollars. DOT school of hard knocks.

Log book unsatisfactory, grounded 24 hrs.
minimum fine 150 dollars.
Consider yourself lucky.

Sleeper bunk, flowered sheet, minimum fine
150 dollars, white only, consider yourself lucky.

Port of entry. Bureaucratic error
your problem, long distance calls
your expense, 4 hour delay, consider yourself lucky.

On the road, flashing lights, DOT agent
surprise check, minimum fine
150 dollars, consider yourself lucky.

Different laws, rules and regulations
every state. Hourly changes. Russian Roulette.
Minimum fine 150 dollars.
Consider yourself lucky.

We can, shut down, any truck
any driver, any time, any place.

POLITICALLY CORRECT POLITICIAN

More liberal than any democrat
More conservative than any republican

UNITED STATES DEPARTMENT
OF DING DONGS

Pompous little bureaucrat
    Banty rooster
        Strutting tall
Short, yet
    almost human
        almost round

Arrogant smirk
    papers in hand

Fresh shave and trim
    Shirt starched
        Pants creased
All clean and fresh
    and definitely
        not refreshing

United States Department
    of Ding Dongs

GOVERNMENT

There is
    no government
like
    no government

Honesty is not an equitable policy.
    Alexander the Great

23

COURTS

High or low
too slow.
Win or lose
makes me
feel sick.
Justice for all
what gall.
The greedy
playing god
graft and
corruption.
Above the
Supreme Court
is the highest court
on the 19th floor
a basketball court.

GOVERNMENT BENEFITS

1950
Government benefits
Plus one nickel
would buy
a cup of coffee
Free refills

1990
Government benefits
plus 50 cents
would buy
a cup of coffee
      Sorry
no refills.

1997
Government benefits
plus $1.50
would buy
a cup of coffee
Refills: $2.00

HOT SNOW

Hot snow
oven mud
oven baked
another world
mysterious and
magical
another illusion
Looks like
Hot snow
over mud.
Salt growing
alive and hot
below sea level
Desert snow
another illusion
Death Valley

Hot Snow

PLOWIN SNOW

Several years before I was born, Dad was plowin down south of the church early in the spring. The weather was warm and mild. During the night it snowed several inches. It wasn't very cold, so early the next morning he started up the Model D John Deere and continued plowin. He was of course plowin under that snow.

Late that morning my Grandfather Otis came out from town and stopped him at the end of the field. My Grandfather was quite riled up and told my Dad to quit plowin because plowin under snow would ruin the ground.

For the next 3 years you could see to the row where he'd plowed that snow under.

Twenty years later, Dad was the first to quit plowin farm ground. It took another twenty years & then some for everyone else to quit plowin.

25

COLD

January cold, Nebraska blizzard ragin three days. Howlin winds, snow drifting. Cornstalks, fenced in cattle three miles from home. I knew they'd been standin, ass into the wind, waitin & waitin, not movin during the storm. No water, no feed for three days. I knew they wanted & needed water first, and then feed.

The storm had ended late at nite. I awoke at 4 a.m. to the calm.

The only sound was the crunch of snow under five buckle overshoes. I was thinkin about the recent blizzard that hit the sandhills real hard where lots of cattle had died. After the storm the national guard had dropped hay from helicopters to isolated, starvin cattle. Helped some that had water. Did more harm than good to some that couldn't get water. Feed ain't no help when you're dyin of thirst.

Walkin & feelin the cold, numbness of 30 below. Seein the beauty of snow and frost sparklin in the starlight and beginnin light in the east.

Sun rising, slight breeze toward the sun, colder now.
Cold enough to change the mind.

Cold

A GRAIN OF SAND

An oyster.
The greater
the pain
the bigger
more beautiful
the pearl.

POKER

When I was a kid, penny ante
  later on, quarter limit
extra income, Saturday nite delight.
  I studied the game, odds and all
players too.
  Bright lights, Lost Wages, Nevada
poker table, 7 card stud
  7 seated, 6 players, I dealer
fast game, 10% + down the slot
  the house always wins
6 players, 3 losers, I even steven
  One winner, stood up, stepped out
I stepped in, sat down, three hours
  winnin slow and steady, playing sharp
playin cool, playin to win.
  Lookin good, lookin better, bettin the limit
full house, jacks over sevens, loser
  full house, queens over deuces.
next hand, lookin good, lookin better
  bettin the limit, full house
queens over sixes, loser
  full house, kings over threes.
Next hand, lookin good
  Lookin better, bettin the limit
full house, kings over fives, loser
  full house, aces over fours.
Money gone!
  Full houses, three in a row, all losers.
POKER

GREETING CARD
WRITING OPPORTUNITY

Needed: Easy-to-read
Graduation cards.

OLD GLORY

Red, white & blue proudly waving
beautifuly in the wind.
The flag; red, white & blue.
Red first, dead red, Indians.
Manifest Destiny.
Denying them their place
their way, their life.
Old glory, the flag.
White next, European transplants.
Nationalism, Patriotism, Saluting
Nagasaki, Hiroshima.
No heroes, old men
women and children
blown away by the red white & blue.
Real people evaporated
only a shadow remaining.
Old Glory, young and irresponsible
Vietnam protestors.
White hippies, burning the flag.
Immoral majority, shocked, aghast.
Dirty and unkept hippies, ragged
patched with the red, white & blue.
Such disrespect.
Moral & patriotic Christians
Blue bloods, killing for
continued freedom and other illusions.
Pass a law to protect
the red, white & blue.

WORK

My work is to follow
    my own spiritual path.
Your work is to follow
    your own spiritual path.
All spiritual paths are
    compatible.

28

When we were cleaning out my grandmother's house, getting ready for the auction, we found, behind the old ringer washer, in the basement, a box, dusty with age. In the box was: 5 bars of Bob White soap, 3 bars of P & G laundry soap, 2 bars of Fels-Naptha, 1 box Pittsburgh wallsize, 1 box Magic Washer, and 3 boxes of Dic-A-Doo. I had to write a piece about Dic-A-Doo.

DIC-A-DOO

Dic-a-Doo, Dic-a-Doo
are you too young to
remember Dic-a-Doo?
Dic-a-Doo, Dic-a-Doo
for homes, stores, factories, boats,
hotels, hospitals & restaurants.
Dic-a-Doo, interior and exterior
Dic-a-Doo, complete satisfaction
or refund of money. Guaranteed
by Good Housekeeping.
Dic-a-Doo, Dic-a-Doo
over 69 billion served!
Is there more to Ameriker
than Ronald McDonald?
Caution: Certain grades of flat
chalky paint are easily affected,
even by soap & water. Apply
Dic-a-Doo at a thinner
consistency, wipe off immediately.
Dic-a-Doo, Dic-a-Doo,
Ameriker loves that the Kernal cooks
        try our extra greasy.
Mopping floors - add a cupful
of Dic-a-Doo, it will do wonders
Dic-a-Doo, Dic-a-Doo
I love the earth, I love the sun.
I love the mountains, I love the rain.
I love the rainbow, I love life,
and I don't like the extra greasy either.
Dic-a-Doo, Dic-a-Doo
put it on, wipe it off.
Dic-a-Doo, Dic-a-Doo
are you too young to
remember Dic-a-Doo?

DIC-A-DOO NUMBER TWO

Dic - a - doo 1932
Dic - a - doo 1992
Desert Dog Diner
Pahrump Nevada
T-Shirt
Big letters
Dic - a - doo
I got this shirt
because my belly
sticks out further
than my Dic - a - doo

PRAIRIE GRASS

In the land of grass
    Seasons pass
The winds blow
    the rivers flow
From grass
    comes life
From life
    comes death
All things pass
    and become grass
The winds blow
    the rivers flow
Seasons pass
    In the land of grass
    PRAIRIE GRASS

BUMPER STICKER

Research and test humans
Save animals.

FOOLS AND STOOLS

Damn fools
    sitting on stools
        bar stools.
Legal drugs
    quite visible
Illegal drugs
    quite available
Damn fools
    sitting on stools
        bar stools.
The future
    soon to be
        hanging over
            toilet stools.
Damn fools.
Stools and fools.

REJECT LETTER

THE ELITIST TIMES
4969 North 69th Street
New York, NY 00001

Mr. Joel Randall
Rural Route
Hicksville, NE 99999

Dear Mr. Randall

Thank you for your submission for publication. After careful consideration we are returning your work.

We felt that the kind of people who would like your work would never read our fine publication.

Sincerely,
The Elitist Times

John Q. Stinkfoot
Managing Editor #14

TELEPHONE

When I was a boy we had a telephone on the farm & ranch. It hung on the south wall of the kitchen, just behind where my father sat at the table.

This phone consisted of a big oak box with two bells and a mouthpiece sticking out a foot from the center. Just below the mouthpiece was a shelf for the phone book and making notes. Hanging on the left side was the receiver for listening and on the right side was a crank. The front was hinged on the right and you could open the box and see inside where there were two batteries, wires, magnets and gadgets that made the bells ring and created the magic of hearing and talking with someone far away.

This telephone was fun to use and simple too. Just turn the crank 2 or 3 complete circles to get the operator to personally get anyone not on your party line, in town or long distance. On the line you just cranked the number. Our number was 23, meaning you cranked two long ones and three short ones. We were at the end of the line. Yes, that meant there was 23 telephones on this deluxe party line.

The line was nearly always busy during any reasonable calling time from early morning till late night. It was always in use, someone talking with someone and others listening. Yes, listening, because everyone could hear all the rings made on the line with 23 telephones and 23 families.

Listening, eavesdropping, minding everyone else's business and social life via the telephone was called 'rubbering.' Rubbering was quite popular due to the curious nature of humans and its easy availability.

In that time and place there was no such thing as television. Town was ten miles away and small enough to have the "welcome" sign and "come back again" sign on the same post. This small town certainly lacked all the social activities of the city.

So, most everyone listened to everyone else on the phone, except my father, and he damn seldom used the phone as he didn't want all those people listening to what he said. My mother, of course, rubbered, except when my father was sitting at the table right under the phone. Dad would give her the devil for not minding her own business whenever he caught her.

People in those days didn't have much money, practically none to spend for entertainment, and besides, there wasn't nothing available to buy anyhow. There was no extra charge for rubbering. It was definitely the community's free entertainment. Had there been even a slight charge, Francis Hammons would never have rubbered. Since it was free he was one of the worst offenders along with his sister Edna. She was my favorite aunt and would gladly have paid for all the fun and joy she got listening to the party line.

Crank the crank, make a call and start your conversation and soon to follow was a click, click, a click here and a click there as people picked up their receivers to rubber. They always waited a short time before listening in. Some sort of country social etiquette in a situation that totally lacked it.

One afternoon Bob Moffett called me to go fishing and I remember hearing over a dozen clicks shortly after I answered the phone. Bob said "What I got to say ain't any of your god damn business so hang up your phone." There was a surprising number of clicks as people hung up their phones. Bob then said "You too Jessee (click) and you too Edna (click) and you too Francis (click)."

We then proceeded to have the closest thing to a private conversation that was ever had on the party line of 23 families.

Don't cry over spilt milk.
There's already enough water in it.

POLICE

The police
to protect
and serve.

It is so.

The police
to protect
and serve.

The State.

SCIENCE FICTION SAFETY

A way for writers to comment on government, religion, civilization, etc. to keep from being blackballed, imprisoned, killed, exiled, etc.

Life is between before birth and after death.
Or, life is after birth and before death.

Life consuming life. It is the nature of things; creation, as created.

CORN HARVEST PROFITEERIN
Standin in line, doublin some corn, Farmer doin fine

During corn harvest the lines get real long at the elevators. Some farmers have lived in trucks day & nite. Upon arrival, you wait in line for the scale at the office where they take a sample and test for moisture, weight and foreign matter and dock you accordingly. They tell you where to unload and you drive over there and stand in line some more.

Farmers waitin & visitin, complainin as farmers will about the price of corn, expenses, weather, government, etc., and of course the long lines. Waitin to weigh back empty, get the ticket and go for another load and repeat the waitin game over and over.

Several towns around us have two grain elevators, one at each end of town. One enterprisin young farmer was waitin in these lines at both elevators with the same load of corn, waitin every day, double lines, Double pay.

> Standin in line,
> doublin some corn,
> Farmer doin fine

CAGES AND POETS

Someone has to rattle their cages
    WAKE UP!
My poet friends
    that's you and me
Rattle their cages
    Someone has to do it
Someday, maybe, they'll see
    that the door's open

In the meantime
    WAKE UP!
My poet friends
Someone has to rattle their cages

Cages and poets

THE FRINGE

As long as I can remember, I've had a fascination with the fringe on the chandelier in my Grandmother's home.

Did it start when I was a baby? An infant? The fringe was wirelike, long & gold, always slightly in motion. Others commented on the shape and beauty of the chandelier, rightly so, it had an elegance and essence of its own. Hanging from the center of the room, over the middle of the table where the family ate on holidays and special occasions.

I remember the fringe getting old, a few unraveling, longer than the rest, a few missing. One day the temptation was more than I could resist. I climbed from the chair on to the table and within reach of the magical, beautiful and alluring fringe. Gently touching and examining the fringe up close, my excitement and attention totally focused on the fringe. Vaguely I remember a strand breaking and being scolded by my grandmother.

I didn't play with the fragile fringe again. However my fascination with it continued as it grew older and more fragile, disintegrating with age.

One day, I saw that the old fringe had been replaced with new. As good a substitute as could be obtained. It wasn't the same, shorter and simpler, lacking the glitter and essence that I was so fascinated with all those years. I longed for the old fringe.

Many years passed, I grew-up, moved away. Whenever I visited I appreciated that chandelier, Grandmother's cooking, talking & visiting, the attic, the basement, the latest knitting and crocheting, etc., etc.

The day came when my Grandmother asked me if there was anything in the house I wanted. I replied, "The chandelier with the fringe, but it is part of this house and wouldn't be the same anywhere else, I guess all I really want is all the wonderful memories of you and this old house."

Months after the auction, my wife Mary Rose acquired a few items from my mother, some of which were my grandmother's. I came in and she asked, "What is this beautiful gold thing?" while handing it to me. I couldn't believe it. It was the original fringe from my grandmother's chandelier. Speechless, surprised and deeply touched, I found it difficult to believe that after all these years, here in my hand was the original fringe. More fascinating and beautiful than even I had remembered.

EDUCATION / EXPERIENCE

Education is what you get from reading the small print in a contract. Experience is what you get from not reading it.

PROFESSIONAL WRITER

It took me 15 years to discover that I had no talent for writing, but I couldn't give it up because by then I was too famous.

Robert Benchley

Chasing fame and fortune, forgetting
the love of simple and gentle things.

Most of what you worry about, never happens.

Your thoughts shape your future.

SPANISH & ACOMA

Spanish
Proud Spanish
not Mexican
Spanish.

Acoma
Peaceful
Indian land
Indian people.
Home.

Iron people
Christian newcomers
Surrender demanded
Arrogance unsurpassed
hundreds killed.

Acoma conquered
Onate trials
mere formality
extreme punishment
cruel & barbaric

One foot
all men, chopped off
Elders removed
Children distributed
Spanish families.

Acoma
Catholic blessed
Christian baptized
conquered & converted
Indian slaves.

Spanish
proud Spanish
not Mexican

Spanish!

BIG CITY, BIG CITY

Much glass, some brass
High class, low class.
Drinkin & drugin
Stealin & killin.
Smokin grass
Fake grass, green grass.
No cows, no sheep
Wasted grass
Wasted lives.
Crash & burn
Cut & run.
Pools of blood.
High class, low class
Some brass, much glass,
Big city, Big city.

Cut and run

    Big city, Big city.

MECHANIC

Mechanic
    not quite

more like may-chanic

May fix it
    may not.

ETERNAL LIFE

As the river flows
    into the ocean
We flow
    into eternity
        for the same reason

POETS

Painting words
on the mirror
of your mind

altering consciousness

Poets reflecting
light and shadows

from the
mystery

the
magic
and life

Painting words
on the mirror
of your mind

Poets!

CONTEST WINNER

Our neighbor Ben, an old farmer & rancher, was always enter-
ing contests. After 20 years he finally won the Pet evaporated
milk slogan contest. Here is his winning entry.

I like Pet evaporated milk because -
No tits to pull
no shit to pitch
Just punch a hole
in the son of a bitch.

HARD TIMES

Hard times, can be cheap, but, not easy.

BIG SIGN

Big Sign, small place
Big Ranches, cows all around
Big Sign, we are
This property and me
Proud to be, cattle free
Big Sign, small place, Big Sign.

MONEY

Money
Frog skins
not quite
paper pictures
of men
Bureaucrats
dead bureaucrats
syphilis, gonorrhea
alcoholism

Slave owners
Killers
Indian killers
Heroes
well paid
money
U.S. Federal
Reserve notes
In God
    we trust
All others
    pay cash
money
no smiles
no gold
no silver
no frog skins
paper heroes
money honey

money

TOBACCO

Legal drug
readily available
advertising slick

Makes u sick
when u try it
Dirty trick

Satisfies no
normal need
Just doesn't click

Makes us sick
and an addict
real quick

Legal drug
readily available
advertising slick

ANTIQUE BUSINESS

The antique business has been so good
that the manufacturers just can't keep up.

HIGH SCHOOL REUNION
OR
AM I THAT EASY TO FORGET?
OR
HITTING THE MAILBOX

High School Reunion 30 years
Mary Rockerfeller
First date
She forgot we ever met
Am I that easy to forget?
Mary Rockerfeller
    Quiet and reserved
    Brother Carl
    Wild and crazy
Home on leave
    Drinking beer
    Cruising back roads
    Throwing empty bottles
    At the mailboxes
    Missing at 40 MPH
By God I'm gonna
    Hit one, slow down
    And pull over closer
    He leaned out the window
    Empty bottle in hand
    It's a good thing
    I slowed down

He sure did hit it
    Sound of broken glass
    Real swearing
    With cries of pain
    Empty bottle in hand
    He never threw it.
Brother Carl
    Wild and crazy
    Mary Rockerfeller
    Quiet and reserved
First date
She forgot we ever met.

AM I THAT EASY TO FORGET?

MOM'S BARGAIN COAT

It wasn't for her, it was too big, besides it was a man's coat. Ugly enough that it didn't sell in season, after season, sale rack or on the clearance rack.

In late July it was on final clearance for a song. Mom, of course bought it and gave it to me in mid afternoon when I came in for a drink of water. The temperature was over a hundred with the humidity close behind. Not even a slight breeze. It was as calm & still as only windy Nebraska can get on a hot humid day in late July.

It was the biggest, heaviest coat I'd ever held, not to mention the ugliest dark brown I'd ever seen. Mom said "try it on". My arms got lost in the sleeves and it nearly drug on the floor. She admitted it was a little "big" but you'll grow into it. I went back to work and soon forgot about that coat.

Years later, early in the spring on a cold, cloudy, windy day we were in the field freezing on them old tractors. This was long before fancy cabs with heating, AC, stereos and padded luxury.

I had on 2 pairs of jeans , 2 shirts, a jacket and a coat, a winter cap down over my ears. So many clothes I could barely move, yet unbearably cold. This was, of course, long before fancy insulated clothing hit the farm and ranch market.

I came in at noon for dinner and started digging thru the closet on the back porch looking for something warm to keep out the cold when I discovered Mom's bargain coat. It was a shock to see it again, uglier and browner than I'd remembered. Like I said earlier, I was more than cold so I tried it on over the coats I already had on. It fit pretty good as I'd grown quite a bit and all them clothes under it made me several sizes bigger than I really was. From them on, whenever it was very cold that coat got used.

When I moved from the farm to Phoenix over 30 years ago, that bargain coat was very worn and dirty. It was again forgotten, hanging in the closet on the back porch.

Recently on the radio, I heard "Coat of Many Colors" by Dolly Parton and it reminded me of Mom's bargain coat and those old memories. Dolly, even with her vast real estate could easily of worn that old coat.

INDIAN OWNERSHIP OF LAND

The land -- belongs to the first who set down on his blanket - which he has thrown down on the ground, and till he leaves it, no other has a right.

Tecumseh

HONOR

Whites achieve honor accumulating possessions
Indians achieve honor giving away possessions.

Life is, but a movement of shadow,
running across, the Earth, disappearing into the sunset.

You have to break some eggs to make an omelet.

EATING YEAVES

Our grandson Patrick's eyes were wide open with astonishment as he asked "you and grandpa eat yeaves?" Mary Rose answered "why yes Patrick, they're really good." Where did you get them yeaves? We got them down at the grocery store this morning. They looked really good and fresh. Would you like to try some when they are ready? Patrick studied them in the pan and thought for a few moments and replied "I guess I'll try just one."

Dinner was soon ready and we put several on our plates and one on our grandson's. It was laid out flat, nearly covering his entire plate. Large and green with lots of red in it. We started eating ours as Patrick watched, making sure we really did eat these strange yeaves.

Patrick took a small bite, didn't make any faces as he chewed it up and swallowed. He ate the whole thing without saying anything. Shortly after he'd finished, I asked him if he liked it. It's OK I guess.

When my grandson was almost finished with the rest of his dinner, I asked him if he would like some more Red Chard. He replied I'm kinda full, and that one was pretty big, so I don't want anymore.

From one extreme to another,
for so long, that now, moderation seems extreme.

Yes, there is a Santa Claus, and an Easter Bunny,
and a Tooth Fairy, and yes, there are
smart Cowboys.

WELDING ROD PORCUPINE

High School Vocational Agriculture Shop. Tuesday and Thursday for two hours of sawing, hammering, welding, grinding and goofing-off.

I don't know who started it or how it came about, but the game caught on real fast and went for a long time starting in the fall and running into spring.

We would grind a point on the end of a welding rod and throw it up to the ceiling when the instructor was occupied a safe distance away. With proper skill the welding rod would stick and stay in the wood ceiling. Without the proper timing and skill it would naturally come back down again. Like I said earlier this game went on for a long time even spreading to the other classes, resulting in the ceiling looking like some kind of oversized porcupine.

One spring day Bangs (the Ag teacher) was demonstrating how to hammer out a plow lay by heating it up red hot and having a student hold it on the anvil with giant tongs while he hit it with a big sledge hammer. All was going well and he was sweating and puffing from all that hard work and heat from the torch and red hot iron. It was on the second go around and about the tenth sledge hammer hit when there was a distracting sound nearby of something hitting the concrete floor.

Well Bangs heard it and looked over that direction and didn't see anything. He continued explaining proper technique and all in hammering out plow lays. He then proceeded to hammer some more and on about the fifth blow something hit him on the back and bounced onto the floor. You of course know what it was, from you know where. Well, Bangs picked up the welding rod, carefully examined it and looked up and sure enough, he discovered the welding rod porcupine. Guess what we did the rest of the morning?

47

ILLEGAL SOUVENIR

August 1st 1992 my P.O. box empty, except this yellow notice U.S. postal service (the term service used very loosely) mail pickup notice please give this notice to a clerk during regular business hours. We are holding some of your mail for the reason, reasons indicated below.
>nothing marked
>nothing indicated
>unmarked possibilities
>Article too large for box
>Too much mail to fit in box
>Postage due
>mail requires a signature

Mystery mail being held, Stand in line, patience test. Postal clerk, tired & slow, took notice and said "I'll be right back", much later returns empty handed and asked "Did you already pick it up?" I reply "no" He said "I'll look some more" much later returns again and said "I can't find anything, are you sure someone didn't pick it up?" I reply "I didn't pick anything up, is it possible you sent it back? The clerk replies "the notice is dated 7/28 someone must of already picked it up," Hands me the notice and said "If something turns up you'll get another notice."

Illegal souvenir

SEEDS LIKE THESE

In cell & Cloister, in monastery & synagogue,
Here one fears hell, another dreams of paradise.
But he who knows the true secrets of his God,
Has planted no such seeds within his heart.
Omar Khayyam, Sufi

THE FEUD

Long time burning
　The fires of hell
Family and friends
　Feeding the fires
of anger, hate and ego

The cause, long ago
　mostly forgotten
It was such a small matter
　Thievery and politics
　　some say
　a woman
　　others say
Memories vague
　in the generations
　　of war, death & suffering
Started long ago

Long time burning
　the fires of hell

Long time burning
　The Feud

REALITY

Martin Luther King said "I have a dream."
but we Indians didn't have a dream. We had a reality.
Ben Black Elk

Too many have strayed from the path
shown by the Great Spirit.
Sequichie Grandfather

DRAWN

I was drawn
    before turning
        looking & seeing
more powerful
    more accurate
        more exiting
Then radar, older too
    I was drawn
        I turned
            looked & saw
                Beauty and more
                    tall & proud
    More striking
        than words
            and feelings
    Suspended
        in the magic
            of the moment
    That melted
        the past
            the future
    Down, into now
    Drawn

As a child I understood how to give; I have forgotten
this grace since I became civilized.
Ohiyesa

We are part of the Earth, and the
Earth is part of us.
Seattle

DOWNTOWN

Yesterday downtown
beggar, panhandler, dirty bum.
Ragged and unkept,
scars from the hard life.
Alcohol & drug problem, more problems.

Avoid 'em, don't talk to 'em
don't look at 'em. Don't see, don't feel.
Don't give, be hard.

Didn't know I wasn't feeling yesterday.
Down town today another beggar, panhandler.
Homeless, hard times, pain, scars.
Many problems, many problems, reaching out.
Begging, panhandling.

I see, I talk, give.
I feel sadness today.

Downtown.

THE GREAT CIVILIZATION

The great civilization
      superior in character
         and quality.
A remarkable heritage
      Astutely aware
         of survival and balance
            and many things
               of eminent importance.
The great civilization
      has been going
         downhill recently.
Ever since
      The European Invasion
         of what is now
            called America.

The Great Civilization

51

COWBOY POETRY GATHERING

Lots of good poetry, stories & music
More than a lot of fun
For you, me and my hon

Clothes I couldn't believe
Even a greenhorn wouldn't wear
And hippies couldn't bear

Fancy high top boots
Never been worn
In recycled corn

Experience exaggerated
From the gifts received
Humorous truth perceived

We enjoyed our parts
My wife and I
This natural high

Old and new friends
Time sure did fly
Hard to say good bye

CONTENT

We were content to let things remain as
the Great Spirit made them.
Chief Joseph

BRAINS

People have just enough brains
to tan their hides, same as
the rest of the animals.

COWBOY BOOTS

TODAY
City slickers
   in style
Pointed toes
Cowboy boots
No spurs

On the dance floor
Multicolored
50's delight.
No horses
No cows
No shit
Clean & shiny.
Vintage
   for sure.
Drugstore
Cowboys.

YESTERDAY
Cowboy boots
Wyoming
Ranch hands
Put 'em on
Took 'em off
   in the barn
Left 'em hanging
with the saddle.
Cowboy boots
Spurs, too.
Workin' horses
Workin' cows.
Boots fit
the curved
Wooden stirrups.
No glamour
No color
Real shit
Real cowboys.

CITY WALK

Cherry Creek and Quebec.
        Denver, Colorado.
Townhouses, condos
        middle class plus.
Orderly and nicely painted
        manicured shrubs & lawns.
Walking is hard
        concrete and asphalt everywhere.
People wearing coats
        driving away in cars.
Everything in style here
        technology and civilization.

Walking toward Cherry Creek
        an oasis in the city desert.
The sound of running water
        music and medicine for me.
Watching & feeling the glistening flow
        snakelike, slithering downstream.
Two bluejays, noisy & playful
        natural beauty, jumping & moving.
Flying downstream, a surprise
        they both dive, water splashing.
Only a moment, onto a limb
        shaking, dancing & singing.

They fly, disappearing
        a blessing, a gift.
I am thankful
        it is good to be here.
Bicycle and motorcycle prints
        people and dog tracks.
Looks like deer tracks.
        no it can't be.
More deer tracks, no doubt
        traveling east, upstream.

Where did they come from?
Where are they going?
From the mountains to the west?
Across the big city?
Moving with the natural rhythms
part of the great mystery.

T.V.

When a guest arrives
to view or not to view
that is the problem.
When a meal is served
to view or not to view
that is the problem
To view or not to view
football or soap.
A population focused
on T.V.
that is the problem.
What a dilemma
what a problem.
What a problem
oh what a problem.
No T.V.
No problem.

We don't have a T.V.

TELEVISION

24 hours a day, 7 day a week
365 days a year
Hundreds of channels
TV summary
"Nothin On"

IRS REJECT

I was out of work
children hungry
their mother
impatient and worried
our money gone.

I applied for a job
Internal Revenue Service
Application completed
my resume attached
Monday tests
Wednesday interview

Everything was looking good
        and then
They found out
that my parents
were married

IRS reject

KISSES & SCARS

My favorite scars
        Kisses & Scars
From the Goddess
of the hard life.

Judging foolishly by income and/or possessions.

One drop of water is as complete
in itself as the ocean.

GUN SHOW

Gun dealers, Gun collectors
Gun nuts, Guns, Guns

Macho men, Rednecks
no dopers, some ropers

Smokers, drinkers
macho shit kickers

Black hats, Blue jeans
Big buckles, Boots

Macho men, Small talk
Men's talk, Money talks
Bullshit walks.

Experts, here & there,
jerks everywhere
beer and cheer, stay clear.

War veterans, casualties, heroes
wounds seen, wounds unseen.

I'll give you a special deal
sorry, no honey, give me, your money.

Gun runners, hustlers, serious
they don't know, its all a joke,

Like kill 'em all
let God sort 'em out.

Appropriately used, the power from
and of prayer can do anything.

OJO LINE EXTENSION

Ole', Ole' 5,000 dollars Stud fee.
Best in the west. Bare the mare.

Ole', Ole', Ojo Line Extension
Ugly damn towers. No need just greed.

Electricity, electricity to the cities
Electricity, electricity ole', ole', money honey.

PNM (Public Miss Service Co. of New Mexico)
Not the best in the west. Already flunked the test.

50,000 dollars stud fee. Corruption Commission
stud service, Bare the customer. Ole', Ole'.

50 mile slice Valle Grande pristine, beautiful.
Sacred shrines, mostly forgotten.

Ole', Ole', Ojo Line Extension
ugly damn towers, No need, just greed.

BIA - Bossing Indians Around
Bureau of Indian Assault, promoting Indian abuse
graft and corruption. Ole', Ole'.

LANL, DOE, PNM
Los Alamos National Lab, Dept. of Energy
Public Service Co. of N.M.
Strange bedfellows. Stud fee, negotiable.
Ole', Ole'.
Against ojo line extension, 19 Indian pueblos
Attorney generals office, Energy Conservation groups
Environmentalists, Naturalists, Rancher Wilsons
You and Me and the SSS (Sacred Shrines Society)

Ojo line extension, ugly damn towers.
No need, just greed.
ole', ole'.

2 FEET, 5 MILES

2 feet from hell
5 miles from heaven
2 feet and 5 miles
from where he was
5 miles from anywhere
2 feet from nowhere
5 miles from there
2 feet from here
Mind long gone
like a turkey in the corn
2 feet from somewhere
5 miles from everywhere

2 feet 5 miles

10% MARKUP

In business
math minor
business major
college graduate
10% educated.

10% markup
easy
just move
the decimal
one place
to the right.

We buy 'em
for $10.00

We sell 'em
for $100.00

10% markup

ANNIE OVER

Annie over
Annie over
Red Rover, Red Rover
go on over
40,000 dollars
Land Rover, Land Rover
White collars, more dollars

Annie over, Red Rover
in the clover
Where's Red Rover?
Red Rover, Red Rover
come on over
Land Rover, Land Rover

Red Clover, Red Clover
Annie over, Annie over
Red Rover, Red Rover
Is it over?
Is it over?

THE AMERICAN DREAM

Chasing
the American dream
more education
more status
more money
more property
more power
more toys.
Chasing
the American dream
that which
really existed
before
they came
to chase
the American dream.

BEAUTIFUL

I was struck
    by the beauty
So very black
    Gold threads glissening

Arizona
    mountain desert
        high timber
            nearly stepped
                on it.

I was struck
    by the beauty
So very black
    Gold threads glissening
        diamond shaped

Timber rattler

Beautiful

ASTUTE OBSERVATION ART SHOW

Art gallery
    recent visit

many pieces
    of art.

Same title

DO NOT TOUCH

The problem with blending the Indian and European cultures
is that the Indians is devoted to living and
the Europeans to getting.
John Ross McIntosh

SAVED AGAIN
Winter 1955 High School Vocational Agriculture Shop Day.

Lowell and I were out behind the shop cutting up an old car frame to make a post hole digger. We were using the acetylene outfit to do the cutting. It was an antique even then, heavy and huge. Steel wheels, big in rear and small in front, a large tank, the apparatus to adjust and mix the acetylene powder and water, an oxygen tank, gauges hoses and torch.

Bud Stall used to steal the acetylene powder, pour some in a fruit jar with a rock and punch some holes in the lid. When thrown into the water it became a bomb, exploding and sending water shooting high into the sky. Bud would then gather up the fish to eat. They were a welcome change from their diet of illegal ducks and geese. Bud demonstrated why the acetylene outfit had a warning sign on it. This was back in the days when warning signs were damn rare, not like today when they are plastered all over everything.

The instructor Bangs was the only one allowed to add the dangerous powder. He also told us about the entire building that was blown up when one had been accidentally upset, killing three people.

Back to Lowell and I, we had carefully rolled this rig out the front door and around the north side of the building. We were behind the shop cutting up this old car frame, generally having a good time as kids will do. The instructor mostly stayed inside to watch and supervise all the teenagers sawing, hammering, welding on all the various projects.

We heard the bell ring, time to clean up and put everything away. Well, we decided there was time for another smoke, beings we were out of sight and all. We were just talking and jiving when someone yelled at us to hurry up it was time to leave. We had goofed-off too long again as usual.

We both started pushing this big heavy rig around the building on the run, sliding around the NW corner of the building on the concrete, we hit a seam in the driveway and over she went, crashing hard right by the door. Damn quick without thinking we grabbed a hold and set her upright, turned white as ghosts knowing the danger and the size of the bomb.

To our surprise nothing happened. After a moment we rolled it very carefully inside as if nothing had happened. Saved again by the angels of damn fools.

ARTISTS CYCLE

Artist
Tacos
New Mexico
Northern
Mountains

Winters
Snow & cold
Artist cutting
And gluing
Pictures
On the walls

Summers
Sunny and warm
Building on
Another room
More walls
For Winter
And the

Artists cycle

I'm free, but, it'll cost ya!

AIN'T NO FAT IN FREEDOM

Wanna live free?
What price
    you willin
        to pay?

You all thinkin
    About money, Honey.

You're in the wrong park
    the freedom park
        is way over yonder.

See that coyote
    she knows
        about freedom.

Survivor
    extermination wars
        waged by man
            unfree and ignorant.

Coyotes and freedom
    both a bit lean
        movin fast
            always alert.

Coyote craftiness
    balancing survival
        and freedom
With, whatever it takes.

There ain't no fat in freedom

THE REAL REASON
COWBOY & RANCHERS GET MARRIED

To have someone to open the gates

COWBOY MAINTENANCE, HORSES, & PICKUPS

Checks the horses
First thing every mornin
Last thing every nite
Checked the pickup
Just last month
When a wheel fell off
Feeds the horses
First thing every mornin
Last thing every nite
Oiled the pickup
Just last week
Red light a blinkin
Repaired the tack
new leather
carefully sewn
Repaired the pickup
Just yesterday
Muffler a draggin
Bob wire
And that's cowboy maintenance
Horses & pickups

THE BLANKET OF TIME

Old age is nothing
but living and leaving
youth behind

Old age is nothing
but remembering, the lessons,
the pain, the joy, the fear
the fun, the journey
of living and leaving
youth behind

Old age is nothing but

The blanket of time.

THIS FEATHER IN MY CAP

You all ask about this feather in my cap. Why? What kind is it?

Well my friends - It's a City Dove
A cousin to the turtle Dove
Now the Dove - is a symbol of peace
to avoid war - to end war
Well - I want to bring it down
home to you, my friend
May you have peace
peace in your heart
peace in your soul
peace in your mind
peace in your life
peace in your family
peace in your community
peace in your world
and may you have love, my friend.

Preachers, priests, and popes
politicians and presidents
pretending prim
and they can't fly
and a pigeon can
and does
and they are beautiful
and now you know
a city dove is
a pigeon
and now you know
a little about
this feather
in my cap

PARADISE

Paradise is in Kansas
Just look at your maps
Drive right into paradise

DAM SITE

Mid way between Albuquerque and El Paso on the Rio Grande, city gal said "in the middle of nowhere" near Hot Springs renamed Truth or Consequences after the Radio show.

Dam Site Recreational Area, restaurant & Lounge. Lakeside dining in a casual atmosphere. U must be 21, to consume alcoholic beverages! In the bar, in the restaurant, or on the patio.

Sunday evening, on the patio, Dutton Swartz Blues Band, Dam Site, dam fine blues. Fire in the barrel, dancing all around.

Welcome to, the Dam Site, best view, best dining, dam rite. No glass allowed, on the patio, no picnicking allowed, on picnic tables, no booze allowed, past the gate.

Marina, Cabins, boat rentals, beach wear, fishing - picnic supplies, beer - ice, water toys, boys will be boys.

Rolling rock, Elephant Butte, extra pale, horse head, premium beer, 1939 poster. Pool tables, no one under 21, allowed to play, the management. Dam Site, proud to be, your bud, dam rite.

The American Bald Eagle, endangered species, protected by, alarm services, Las Cruces. No pets allowed, shoes required, shirt required, pants forgotten. Ring buzzer, for assistance. Fraternal Order of police, New Mexico Sheriffs & Police Association, Chamber of Commerce.

You check is welcome, collectrite system, Mary Sweet, 1991, Sweet Mary.

Dam Site
      This Business is
        Consumer preferred
        Dam Rite.

DO OR DON'T?

Any decision made easy
If it feels good in your heart before
    doing it
If it will feel good in your heart while
    doing it
If it will feel good in your heart after
    doing it
Then do it

If it don't feel good in your heart before
    doing it
If it won't feel good in your heart while
    doing it
If it won't feel good in your heart after
    doing it
Then don't do it.

EDUCATION PHASE TWO

What I knew
    for sure
        long ago
            from school

Much delayed
    my learning
        and understanding

Of what
    I now know
        From life

Education
    Phase Two

PAIN ERASED

Old age
    near death
        much pain

Pain erased
    by Healing shadows

E. T.

Eyes asparkle
    more bounce
        per ounce

Quick humor
    very bright
        poet's delight

In my dreams
    some caught
        more thoughts

Special gift
    seldom blue
        Hycoo too

Easy smile
    accepts life
        with strife

Evelyn Terry
    sweeter than
        any berry

Eternity is now, so is love.

WE'RE CALLING

We're calling
 we're calling.
Little People
Ancient Ones
 calling, calling.

Listen, listen
 You, yes, you
 listen, listen.

We're here
 waiting, waiting, for you.
Cooperate, cooperate
 with your heart, with us.

Little people, Ancient Ones
 your life, your work.
All life

We're calling, we're calling.

WE'RE CALLING

100 YEARS OF COWBOY PROGRESS

100 yrs ago: Horses hauled cowboys around 90 percent of the time.

Today: Cowboys haul horses around 90 percent of the time.

She was an earth angel, her mother was a
heavenly angel bred by the devil.

70

SPRING, THE WIND

It was calm at sunrise, soon a slight breeze gently dancing with the trees. Gradually increasing. Within an hour it was windy, dust blowing, trees bending. Uncomfortable to be, see and breathe.

Welcome the spring, the "power," trees and plants growing. Everything becoming more awake, more alive.

The wind bringing the summer from the south, pushing the winter back home to the north, and as they collide it is spring. Winter hanging on, summer pushing in. Battle raging - hot days, cold days, cloudy days, sunny days, windy days.

Winter knowing it must give in to summer, yet hanging on, resisting the inevitable. The power of the wind bringing summer must prevail for all life.

SEX

From the mystery
life comes
thru sex.
No sex
no life.
Creation.
Mystery.
Sexual energy
creation
natural cycles
and rhythms.
Healthy & beautiful
sexuality.
Repressed
oppressed
then obsessed.
Sexual abuse
sexual abusing.
Now we're moving
into the mystery
of spirituality and
sexuality.

WILLOW

I remember
    when it happened
        behind schedule
In a hurry, late
    shortcut
Shade tree
    There you were
        There we were
        connection
        Beyond time
I knew
    you knew
It was wonderful
    a gift
That weekend
    together
We parted
    lives to live
        apart
yet together

Beyond time
Willow

CHINESE INVENTIONS

Fireworks - 700 years ago
Cards - 1000 years ago
Paper money - 1200 years ago
Fishing reel - 2000 years ago
Wheelbarrow - 2050 years ago
Paper - 2150 years ago
Kites - 2300 year ago
Umbrellas - 2400 years ago
Parachutes - 2100 years ago

EASY CATCH

Escaped criminal

The easiest
    to catch
        are Mexicans

They always
    go home
        to their mother

Easy Catch

WATER FALL

Falling water
Flowing
Bubbling.
Dreamy sounds
    of ancient
Voices murmuring
        messages
        from the
        Spirits.
Become still
    and listen
    to sounds
    of bubbling
    flowing
Falling Water.

Religious orders have enough religion
    to war against each other.

OUR STORY

We are born
    hearts open
      we know
        we are divine.
We poop
    this reality
      we forget
        we are divine.
Anger, fear
    we absorb
      we deny
        we are divine.
Pain and shame
    our heart hardens
      we deny
        the divine.
So young
    so miserable
      so sad
        it is hell.
Escaping, escaping
    running, medicating
      no feelings
        no life.
Compulsions, addictions
    more & more pain
      hitting bottom
        seeking help.
Support group
    surrendering
      feeling & changing
        sharing & caring.

Inner child
reparenting
nurturing & supporting
growing & healing.
Supporting ourselves
supporting the group
supporting the process
we are divine.
Finding our path
slipping & sliding
facing our fears
we are divine.
Spiritual blessings
opening the heart
remembering we are divine
we are divine.

EASY

Wanna hurt
a white man?
Indian Instructions
Easy-
Just take
his
last dollar
and listen
to him
hollar.

John Wayne was a collector of dolls.

VICTIM

As a baby my parents
abused me.
I was a victim.
As a child my teachers
abused me.
I was a victim.
As an adult my bosses
abused me.
I was a victim.
I tried to escape
fantasy, drugs, sex, running.
I was a victim.
I misunderstood myself & life
apathy, inertia, depression.
I was a victim.
I admitted I needed help.
Searched, thought & sought.
Tired of being a victim.
I found my spiritual path.
I began recovery
learning a better way.
A victim less & less.
I continue to heal, recover & grow,
living new and better ways
opportunities more & more.
I am following my spiritual path
guided by my higher powers.
A victim no more.

MOTHER-IN-LAWS

Most men like their wives' mother.
Most women don't like their husbands mother.

Over 50 % of Americans would like to lose weight.

LAW

"Seek not the law in your scriptures, for the law is life, whereas the scripture is dead. I tell you truly, Moses received not his laws from God in writing, but through the living word. In everything that is life is the law written. You find it in the grass, in the tree, in the river, in the mountain, in the birds of heaven, in the fishes of the sea; but seek it chiefly in yourselves. For I tell you truly, all living things are nearer to God than the scripture which is without life. God so made life and all living things that they might be the everliving word, teach the laws of the true God to people. God wrote not the laws in the pages of books, but in your heart and in your spirit. They are in your breath, your blood, your bone; in your flesh, you bowels, your eyes, your ears, and in every little part of your body. They are present in the air, in the water, in the earth, in the plants, in the sunbeams, in the depths and in the heights. They all speak to you that you may understand the tongue and the will of the living God" Jesus answered.

Translated from an ancient Aramic manuscript in the Vatican library in Rome by Dr. Edmond Szekely.

This is a reverse anthropological interpretation by Grey Rabbit.

PLEDGE OF ALLEGIANCE

We pledge allegiance
to Mother Earth
and to the life
which she supports.
Many universes
under Spirit
indivisible
with love
sharing and respect
for all.

77

This came from the Indian war cry "It is a good day to die."

IT IS A GOOD DAY TO LIVE

It's a good day to live
to work, to play.
It's a good day to live
to laugh, to cry
to feel, to learn.
It's a good day to live
to remember
to celebrate life.
It's a good day to live
to let go of yourself
to open your heart.
It's a good day to live
to love, share, and respect.
It's a good day to live
to continue the magical
journey from the mystery
back to the mystery.
It is a good day to live.

POSSIBLE MARRIAGE
PARTNER WARNING

You are attracted to partners that will repeat & continue your families patterns of behavior, especially the problem ones.

KNOWING DIFFERENCE

Knowing in the mind is different than
Knowing in the heart.

Ordinary is sacred

FARAWAY EYES

Wrinkled with age
Old you see.

Faraway eyes
lost in time
Eighteen
in love.
Remembering
the pain,
a silent
tear falls.

Living and loving
All over again.
The years,
too few,
too fast.

Close your eyes
and see.

Faraway eyes.

It seems to me that the rulers of the Cherokees have sufficient intelligence to the see the utter imbecilty of placing any further reliance upon the Supreme Court.

Governor Wilson Lumpkin
Georgia, 1831

We can get over being poor, but it takes longer
to get over being ignorant.
Jane Sequichie Hifler

NO

No Indian blood
on our side
of the family.
Cherokee land claim.
No, we don't want
to talk about
the past.
Grandfather hung
by the KKK.
No, it wasn't
popular
to be
an Indian.
No Indian blood
on our side of
the family.
Choctaw chuckle
No, that's your
imagination
running wild.
No, we don't
talk about
sexual abuse either.
No Indian blood
on our side
of the family.
some on your father's side.
No Indian blood
on our side
of the family.

Are not women and children more timid than men?
Tonkahaska

IN THE DARKNESS

It was close to new moon and getting dark. We were only a couple of miles from the canyon with the cliff dwellings, a bit tired and in good spirits. We talked of the land, the people, and earlier times. The past, present and future of these New Mexico mountains & valleys. The Indians, the Spanish, the Anglos and the struggles today.

We arrived at the cliff dwellings in darkness, awed by the clear skies and the number of stars we could see.

We crawled into a cliff dwelling into total darkness. We sat in silence, at rest for awhile adjusting to the darkness & stillness. It was pitch dark and we could not see a thing. Perhaps a half hour passed and I began to notice three indistinguishable shapes about a foot high at eye level on the back wall.

I asked my friend if he could see them and he said "Yes, they seem to have a slight glow to them." I agree. We continued to sit in the darkness and look, feeling somehow drawn to the three objects we were unable to really identify. My friend crawled out of the cave and returned with a flashlight. When he turned it on, we saw a shelf that was carved into the back wall. The shelf was totally empty. When we looked closely in the dust, there were three circles where long ago the three kachinas stood.

LITTLE ONE

Putting wood in the stove.
Fast movement.
What is it?
Little one
where did you come from?
Long tail
4 legs.
Baby lizard
stuck in the carpet.
Where did you come from?
Little one.

P.O.

Santa Fe
Main
4 o'clock
Thursday
long line
20 count
not moving
bureaucracy
moving slow
2 clerks
1 disappears
anger
resentment
monopoly
line not moving
S O B
irritating
never returned
people in line
unhappy faces
discontented
complaints
years & years
no change
my error
some change
longer lines
higher wages.

LADY LOVE

After the storm
   she moved on
      like the weather
Love changes everything
    and everything changes
      - Even Love -

Follow your heart
but
Keep your Head.

FOREVER

How long
is forever?

Forever is
as long
as it lasts

How long
is forever
this time?

Forever.

FOUND POEM

Sedona
Arizona

NOTICE

All children
running loose
and unattended

Will be
towed away

and stored

at owners expense.

GET A LIFE

You've heard it
I've heard it
Get a life
Here's How!
Check out
of the cities
and bars
Check into
the outdoors
mother nature
Move out of
the illusion
of progress
Move into
the truth
of mother nature
Soak up
Father Sun
Grandmother moon
A new day
walk upstream
a new way
Let the past go
Look to the future
Be in the present
You've heard it
do it
make a change
Get a life

Again - I recall the great vision you sent me.
It may be that some little root of the sacred tree still lives.
Black Elk 1912

GOOD ADVICE

Confused?
Don't know what to do?
what's right?
What's wrong?
What will work?
won't work
confused?
Can't divide?
Simple solution
Simple recommendation
Good Advice
Works nearly all the time
Any situation, any problem
short term
long term
Simply do
the opposite
recommended by
Government and/or Religion

Good Advice

HOT AND ICY

Driving into
Phoenix
mid day
July
110 degrees

Big billboard
announcing
icy conditions
ahead
79 cents
Hot and Icy

THE RIDE

Old truck
    rusted & faded
        worn tires.
Early morning
    on the road
        getting acquainted.
He's hungover
    sugar, coffee
        smoking cigarettes.
I see him
    myself long ago.
        Lingering sadness.
Radar detector,
    pedal to the metal
        speeding, speeding.
Off the pavement
    adrenaline rush.
        NOW - he's alert.
Mountains - grass
    wheat - corn
        farms - towns.
13 hours, 700 miles
    no wrecks, no cops.
        Grateful I'm home.
I wished him well
    paid him extra
        he's speeding on.

The white men & Indians kept fighting each other
backward and forward, and then
I came in and made peace myself.
Santana

WRITING FROM THE HEART

Layers and shadows
Inspiration reflecting
Beyond the illusions
Softened some
by the cold
Hard facts of life
My writing
becomes
a window
Into the mystery
Expanding my heart
Consuming my being
The eagle screamed
melting words
into my soul
Beyond reality
into truth
and beauty
No longer
taking life
too seriously
Writing from the heart

LIVING OR WAITING

It is much better to live today
than to wait, for a future time to be happy.

PRAYING, PREYING

There's a difference between praying & preying
Some preachers do both.

Lost and lodged in the material world.

MASSAGE OR MY HANDS

The body
    never lies
    basic need
    to touch
    be touched
    the body
    knows.
My hands
    work easily
    in cooperation
    with
    your body
    your energy
    your essence.
My hands
    surrender to
    the higher powers
    cooperating and
    flowing with
    the mystery
    the magic
    the healing.
My hands
    know.

VULTURES

Vultures have
    the keenest
        sense of smell
of all the birds.

Vultures are
    the most
        appreciative
of the sweetest smell
        of all
    Death.

HOMELESS

Not uptown, downtown
Lackin them dollar bills
and what it takes to ride
the ferris wheel of high society
or the merry go round of looking good
Been in school, been in jail, been around
got a past that won't quit
already learned the difference
between necessities & luxuries
Early morning gathering in the park
from the gutters, alleys, bridges & culverts
young & old, male and female
Ragged & dirty, cold & hungry
Legal & illegal drugs, pain & misery
Gathering up energy and courage
to hustle & beg. Whatever it takes
to make it thru another day
Homeless

JUSTIN CASE

Overweight traveller
Overweight suitcase
It wasn't
the necessities
It was
the
just in case
might need it
Overweight suitcase
Overweight traveller
Justin case

Avoid hurting or harming anyone.

HANDS

Hands
not pans
or glands.
Not any
hands
my hands.
Large, strong
warm, loving.
Magical hands.
Scarred yesterday.
Loved & appreciated
today.
Hands
my hands.
Healing hands
right hand
writing hand
trained hand
use more.
Left hand
used less
trained less.
Yet
sometimes
in places unseen
a keener sense
the left hand
able to do
the impossible.
Regrets
the right hand.
Two hands
look alike
almost
The lines tell
different stories
left & right
my hands.
Hands.

LEAPING

A life of experiencing
A life of lessons
Leaping from
   one dream
      to another
Just say yes
   to your dream
Just say yes
   then
Take a leap
   a leap
A leap of hope
A leap of faith
Leaping from
   one dream
      to another
A life to experience
A life of lessons
Leaping

MAKING LOVE

Chinese man
   one woman
      200 different ways.

Making love

American man
   200 women
      all the same way.

Do not hurt your neighbor,
for it is not him you wrong, but yourself.
The Shawnee

LETTING GO

Letting go
of the old ways
no longer working
Letting go
of fear
of rules
Letting go
of I'm trapped
I can't
Letting go
growing closer
to you
Letting go
growing closer
to me
Letting go
growing closer
to mystery
Letting go

LITE

A splash of lite
in the nite
It was love
at first site
Well, not quite
more like

It was love
at first bite
A splash of lite
in the nite.

It was not
Lite.

LONG GONE

Oh I wonder
    where you are
Last call
    from Arkansas
Long gone
    movin on
My guess
    is west
Less crazy
    less lazy
Oh I wonder
    where you are
Long gone
    like a turkey
        in the corn

Oh I wonder
    where you are

Long Gone

LONG GONE #2

Sorry bride
    I gotta ride
Please understand
    this man
just gotta keep
    these feet
a movin on
    and carryin on
Sorry bride
    I gotta ride
Long gone

RICHARD'S ROOF

Cut one 40 inches
no, 39 and 3/4.
Green house, Green house.
No permit
No women
No sweat.
Dis ain't the White House.
Move the ladder
Get the saw.
Driving nails
big hammer
thumb on ice.
Green house, Blue house.
Adobe house.
Need a hand
over here, over there.
Green house, Green house.
No permit
No women
No sweat.
Dis ain't the White House.

They searched for a long time for the source of life,
and at last came to the thought that it issues from
an invisible creative power to which, they applied
the name Wa-ko-da.
Playful Calf

We never quarrel about the Great Spirit
Cochise

MAJOR PROBLEM

Major problem
  walking thru life

always pushing
  on doors
marked pull.

always pulling
  on doors
marked push.

major problem
walking thru life

major problem

LEAVE IT TO BEAVER

LEAVE IT TO BEAVER

Eliminate
the Army Corps of
Engineers.

LEAVE IT TO BEAVER

This hand is not the color of your hand,
but if I pierce it I shall feel pain.
The blood that will follow from mine
will be the same color as yours.
The Great Spirit made us both.
Standing Bear

A MANS HEART

A man's heart goes
    from soft to hard
        and back to soft
Just like something
    else.

MARRIAGE BY FIRE

Midnight,
the fire
    was high.
Flames dancing.
    the couple,
trusting love
    and fate.
held hands
    and danced
toward the fire.
They danced
into the flames
    and through
        the fire.

Married

Surviving

Marriage by fire.

MARRIAGE VOWS

Old marriage vows
until death
    do'uth part

new marriage vows
until stress
    do'uth part

MODERN MATH

4 times white = black

Doing time
  for crime
     crack
mostly blacks
  20 years

Doing time
  for crime
     cocaine
mostly white
  5 years

4 times white = Black

Modern Math

OLD SYSTEM, NEW SYSTEM

Manifest Destiny

Those who created
This new system
that obviously
   doesn't work
   are
those who destroyed
the old system
tested by time
that obviously
   did work
Manifest Destiny

Old system
   New system

OCEAN SOUNDS

Sounds, sounds
of the ocean.
the water, moving
making sounds
in rhythm
with the universe
Healing sounds
wet sounds
always changing
with the swells
the breaks
rolling and falling.
Sounds of birds calling
flying overhead
Sounds of flight
feathers and air
blending with
the sounds
of the ocean.

RUT

Alarm
dress
breakfast
work
lunch
work
dinner
TV
sleep
rut.

Joy - take it by the hand and walk with it.

ORGANIZATIONS

"Eventually
all organizations
begin to act
like organizations."

Jim Van Cleave
my friend

SAME THING ONLY DIFFERENT

Same thing
only different
So different
yet the same
Almost the same
yet different
Different so different
no different
The same
different name
The same
no different
Same thing
different yet
The same thing
only different

Just like people
same thing
only different.

The Great Spirit placed us here
-to take good care of Mother Earth,
all life, each other and ourselves.

PERFECT AGE

Old enough
　　to have the experience
Young enough
　　to have the vigor
Old enough
　　to know better
Young enough
　　not to care
Perfect age.

TOWARD THE MOUNTAINS

After the storm, after the rain
the Earth is soft and wet
part of the calmness.
To the east, the top of Black Mesa.
To the west, teardrops in the rock.
To the north, green trees & grass.
To the south, ancient wind & water
carvings.

After the storm, after the rain
the birds sing in celebration
part of the peacefulness.

The oneness we long for
The oneness that is
The oneness we are.

Lack of enthusiasm brings on sadness.

PROGRESS IN SUMARA

President McKinley said
"It is our duty
    to uplift, educate
    civilize and Christianize
    these poor people
    of Sumara."

The order came
    kill every
    Sumaran man.

the colonel asked
    the general
    "above what age?"
    he answered "10".

It was done.

Christian soldiers
    Christianized
    Sumara.

Progress in Sumara.

ZEROS

Education
math
    in school
they taught
    me
zeros are
    nothing
So I'll
    trade you
this ten
    for a hundred.

PROGRESSIVE JUDICIAL SYSTEM

Long ago illusion
            presumed innocent
                - until -
                        proved guilty

More recent
            presumed guilty
                - until -
                        proved guilty

Today
        still guilty
            - after -
                        proved innocent
or guilty till proved wealthy

Progress
Progressive Judicial System

PURE AND SIMPLE

I've known love
            pure and simple
I've loved and
I've been loved
            more than nice
I've known lust
            pure and simple
            more than nice
But lust is best
            properly mixed
            with love
Pure and simple

There ain't no sound like a pig gettin cut.

REDNECK FOREPLAY

Get in the truck bitch.

REDNECK RELIGION

If you ain't hereafter
what I'm after
You'll be here
After I'm gone.

ON THE ROAD AGAIN (2)

On the road again
to somewhere
dreamed
The journey
Illusions of time
and distance
Dreams dreamed
Dreams chased
Dreams lived
Arrived again
Arrived and gone
on the road again
Curves and crossroads
All going somewhere
But where?
On the road again
Lifes adventure
to journeys end

On the Road again

Born again Pagan.

This was inspired by Ross Lewallen's sharing during a Thursday lunch (men's group).

ON THE ROAD AGAIN

On the road again
many hours
many miles
hungry.
Road food.
Texas cafe
yellow stains
cigarette smoke
worn upholstery
worn menu
worn waitress.
Tired too.
Boondocks
greasy spoon
local hangout.
300 pounders
good ole boys
shit kickers
whiskey drinkers.
Don't like pinko's
queers, dudes
niggers, jews
or hippies neither.
Don't like
strangers either
especially men
wearing jewelry
hair too long.
Icy stares
whispered whispers
Feeling unsafe
escape
cafe of death.
No dinner.
On the road
again.

RELIGIONS

are
only examples
of societies
meager, abusive
attempts
to become

spiritual.

SAUNA SURVIVED

Death defied
Hot sauna
220 plus
Two bodies
Temperature rising
Movement, sex
Locomotion
Temperatures rising
more heat
More sweat
more risk
More danger
Hearts pounding
Entered the
Twilight zone
Slow motion
no motion
Too hot, too hot
Escape, escape
Death defied
Sauna survived.

No rest for the wicked and
the righteous don't need none.
David Lee (Pig Poet)

SHOP TILL U DROP

Shoppin the mall
10-9 six days a week
Shop till U drop
Isn't for the weak
    Loco locals
    Always at the mall
    Almost a ball
    Shop till U drop
Give it hell every day
Except - Sunday morning
Time off for good behavior
And Church, of course
    Showin off them new duds
    From Shoppin the mall
    Gettin that strength
    To carry on carryin on
Shoppin the mall
Day in and day out
Almost a ball
Shop till U drop

THE WAY IT IS

More or less
more can be less
Less can be more
And that's the way
    It is
More or less

AIRSICKNESS

The real cause of airsickness is the Wright Brothers.

SITTING

My father
sitting
couch, silent room
TV on
picture only
nature program

Elbow propped
head resting
in hand
eyes closed

Head jerks
eyes open
watching again
nature program

Silent room
my father

Sitting

WHITE TRAIL

Naked eye
trail unseen
followed
on horseback
full gallop
Apache boy.

STONEHENGE

Give me that old time religion.

MONEY, HONEY

Lie, steal & cheat.
Do anything & everything
for the money, honey.
House payment
car payment
they want the money, honey.
Bill collector
tax collector
pay the money, honey.
Gas money
lunch money
we need money, honey.
Looking for money
searching everywhere
where's the money, honey?
Get a job
40 hour week
give me your money, honey.
The government wants money
the church wants money.
Keep the money, honey.
Love is money
money is love.
Here's the money, honey.

TRIP TO THE MOON

End to end
50 million a day
Hot Dog
trip to the moon
Every 6 months

Hot dogs
50 million a day
end to end
Every 6 months
Hot dog
Trip to the moon

SOMETIMES

Sometimes
You're in
my dreams

I know
we can't
go back

But
Sometimes still
you're in
my dreams
Sometimes

TEENAGERS

Families, Schools
Churches & Society

Teenagers
their short life
turned upside down
inside out, sideways
crosswise, topsy-turvey
up and down
in and out
over, around
under and thru.

Sex and drugs

Teenagers.

God. is, an abbreviation, for Goddess.

EASY MONEY

40 hour week
payday on Friday
steady job
steady money.
Easy money - almost.
Wear the clothes
punch the clock
time and a half
over 40 hours.
Easy money - almost.
Drive the traffic
fight the pressure
bite the bullet.
Life and soul.
Easy money - almost.
Smile for the boss
kiss ass.
Holiday - double-time
easy money - almost.
Steady job
easy money
almost.
Selling my
life & soul.

FUN

The most important discipline.

We do not take up the warpath without
a just cause and honest purpose.
Pushmataka

THREE O'CLOCK

Three o'clock and I'm wide awake, like yesterday morning except today I get up. The dark, the calm. Thankful for the sleep, the dreamtime. The calm similar to before the storm, yet there is no storm coming. I know at a deep level that it is the calm of death. That time before night ends, before morning begins, that time of death, when life often ends.

TOWN RULE

Great Grandfathers rule: Don't go to town - unless
- you've got something to sell.

WILD

Wild animals
no not wild
natural
natural animals
natural as in nature
Wild
Wild as in civilized
Wild as in people
Wild as in government
Wild as in cities
Wild as in war
Natural animals
natural herds
natural flocks
larger than large
farther than
the eye could see
Killed and destroyed
Wild
Wild White, Christians
Wild

THAT'S THE WAY YOU ARE

Got a big nose, getting bald
    That's the way you are
Too fat, too thin
Too tall, too short
    That's the way you are
Got a little nick in your heart
    that's the way you are
Stretch marks for the ladies
War wounds for the men
    That's the way you are
Too young, too old
Too smart, too dumb
Too fast, too slow
Too worldly, too naive
    That's the way you are
Alcohol & drugs, drunk & stoned
High & low, crash & burn
Rehab & changes, up & uplifting
    That's the way you are
Too manic, too depressed
Got married, lovers or strangers
Male or female, got divorced
Success & failure, lessons learned
Lessons in progress
Lessons forgotten.

    you got, you got
        The way you are!

* Co written with Ross Lewallen & Sweet Sue

AGREEABLE FRIENDS

The most agreeable friends are animals.
They ask no questions,
don't criticize and give unconditional love.

IN AND AROUND L.A.

30 day sentence
San Bernardino to Santa Monica
Pasadena to Santa Ana

N, S, E & W
Smog & more smog

Locals always say
It's pretty good here
   and point
It's worse over there

You can see
   the food you eat
      no complaints
You can see
   the water you drink
   no complaints
   and here
You can see
   The air you breath
   Don't complain
In and around L.A.

STATEN ISLAND TOUR

Garbage towering high
   Giant cranes
      Loading barges
         24 hours a day
Big feast
   Birds galore
      free treats
         mixed and aged
Staten Island Tour
   Worldwide allure
      Breath taking
         Views and smells
It sure is swell
   on the
      Staten Island Tour

IRAN RELIGIOUS CHANT

God is Great, Death to America

A spiritual being, having a human experience.

Las Vegas can easily make you a millionaire --
-- If -- you are a billionaire.

Celebrating prestigious poverty with flea market decor.

May you always be the kind of person
your dog thinks you are.

Jogging - a healthy case of the runs.

HONORABLE

"Honorable" preceding the name of a judge,
Senator and such doesn't necessarily mean they are.

Einstein dreamed the theory of relativity.

THEN & NOW, SINGIN & PICKIN

Some talent
Some practice
more practice
more dreamin
Waitin tables
Workin & waitin
Dreamin & hopin
Singin & pickin
Been near success
Knows some people
Knows some ropes
Stuborn & unbending
Business is Business
Infested with lice
can't or won't
pay the price
Fell in love
years ago
Drov 'em crazy
still does
Times are changin
It ain't no game
Still hangin on
Everythings the same
Loves the music
Knows what it's about
opinionated & particular
won't sell out
Computer concubine
China connection
Smog & traffic
LA weary
Gettin older
Gettin by
It ain't enough
never was

TOO, TOO

Too soon
she said
"I love you."
Too soon
love left
Too late
she left.

Too late
I said
"I love you"
too soon
she said
"I love you"
too late
she left.

Too bad
so sad.

EARTH ANGEL

She was an angel with a broken wing.

PARIS, FRANCE

Dog doo doo and garbage in the streets.

RIGHT OR WRONG

You could be as right as I am
or I could be as wrong as you are.

I WASN'T BORN YESTERDAY

This country bumpkin
been around some
I'm 52.
Gone the mile
both ways
shortcuts
took some.
Grew-up
too fast.
Aging young
detours
too many times
lost
city learned.
Around the block
a time or two.
Aged some
down the alley
and back again
more too.
I wasn't born yesterday.

MARRIAGE EXPECTATIONS

Any expectation beyond companionship
will be a problem.

Pushwater is the Indian word for gasoline.

GIVE AND TAKE

Some days we give more than we take.
Some days we take more than we give.

WALK ACROSS AMERICA

Walk Across America
   that's right
     walk
3,000 miles
one step at a time.

Invitation from
Western Shoshone Indians
to help protest
   the most heavily
bombed nation on Earth.
   Theirs.

Walk Across America
    Walking
Walking in the cold
Walking in the snow
Walking in the heat
Walking in the rain
No, not like Johnnie Rae
    more like
Johnny Appleseed
planting seeds
   seeds of hope
      and change
For all life
for Mother Earth
for native rights
for ending nuclear testing.

Walk across America
Walking a spiritual path
a living prayer
3000 miles long
one step at a time.

Walk across America
   that's right

   Walk

INSPIRATION

In the mountains and at the
seashore you can see, hear and
feel inspiration.

In Nebraska the wind blows
inspiration into every pore
of your body.

ALL NIGHT CEREMONY

In our hearts, to feel the pain, of 10,000 years
In our hearts, to feel the joy, of living life
In our hearts, to feel the hope, of change
Walk across America, 3000 miles
one step at a time to Western Shoshone
prayers & ceremonies, nuclear bombing
All nite ceremony, Shoshone elders
Shoshone land, Shoshone gifts
Loving, peaceful & strong Shashone
Red, white, black, yellow,
Indians, Europeans, Negroes, Orientals
all nite ceremony, Shoshone sharing
A spirit, for all, to see, to feel
Brother owl, magic eyes, bringing wisdom
Brother bear, shinny coat, strength of many
Brother Eagle, piercing reality, courage
On our spiritual path
for all the world to see
Them & us, you & me
Walking across America, 3000 miles
one step at a time to Western Shoshone
prayers & ceremonies, nuclear bombing site

All night ceremony

These two Father pieces were written during the New Mexico Men's Wellness Conference while doing inner child family of origin grief work.

FATHER

My father, the farm, the same.
Anger, work.
Hitting my brother, no hugs.
Macho handshake, squeezing too hard, too long.
Fighting the pain, boys don't cry.
Work, work.
A day. A night. A day.
Every other night, sleep some.
Winter morning, dark and cold.
Whiskey bottle, fire in the belly.
Work, Work, anger, work, anger, work.
Scarred upper lip, broken beer bottle.
Broken hip, no doctor.
Damaged back, missing muscles.
Pain, pain; work, work
pain, work, pain, work, work.
My father.

FATHER, FATHER

Father, father, love me, protect me.
Father, father, teach me, help me
notice me. Father, father
Where are you?
Where are you?
Where are you?
I miss you.
Father, father, I'm working
I'm working harder, harder & harder.
I want your approval.
Criticism, criticism, more criticism.
Never good enough, never enough
never enough. Father, father
I needed your love.
I needed your approval.
I needed your support.
I needed your help.
I needed your attention.
I needed. I needed more.

MY FATHER SAID

"When I was young, some days were better than others. Now I'm old and some days are worse than others."

WORKING MOTHER

Mexican woman
    Hoeing beets
    Hard work

Afternoon heat
    Labor pains
    Shade tree

Mexican Woman
    Hoeing beets
    Catching up

Missed a round
    Baby boy
    in a sling

Working Mother

PARENTS 1990's

Parents in the 90's
    telling kids
        to say no.

When
    they didn't
        In the 60's.

121

GRANDFATHER BLACKSTONE

Orphaned on the Trail of Tears
    Grandfather was Cherokee.
Adopted by the white Methodists.
    Abused by the white Methodists.
Grandfather tried to become white
    lied and cheated, he was smart.
He drank, gambled & swore
    traveled and chased women.
Married, had eight children
    settled down a bit.
Worked for the railroad
    bought a place.
Grandfather couldn't resist
    gambling & women.
Something went wrong
    when my mother was two.
He never came home
    hung by the Ku Klux Klan.
Grandfather was a Cherokee.

RIDING WITH GRANDPA RANDALL

"Grandpa, I want to go faster."
    I said when I was three.
Grandpa speeds up. Later...
"Grandpa, I want to go faster."
Grandpa speeds up. Later...
"Grandpa, I want to go faster."
Grandpa sez, "We're going 60 MPH,
how fast do you want to go?"
    Pause...
"Grandpa, how fast is a bat
    out of hell?"

BREAKING UP

Women initiate the break-up 70% of the time.

GRANDPA 1970's

Small and dark
lean and leathery
In his seventies
working and serving
His people
  all people
   all life
    and me.
In his seventies
  Slow and steady
Every move
  Every word
   Every act
Focused and present
  Efficient
Grandpa
More than teacher
More than friend

Singing water
Sound of water falling
Grandpa

GRANDPA 1991

Showing
the heavy weight
  of age
moving slow
in the distance
  coming closer
moving slow
a bounce
a rhythm
from long ago
moving slow
a bounce
a rhythm
of long ago
moving slow
showing
the heavy weight
  of age
Grandpa 1991

GREAT GRANDPA'S GREAT MOLASSES

They said it was the best and folks came from miles around to buy it. Dollar a gallon for 30 years. When the price was up and everyone else was selling for over a dollar he always said it wasn't worth any more than a dollar.

When the price was down and everyone else was selling for less than a dollar he always said it was worth a dollar same as always.

Well, I don't know if it was the best but I know he always sold all he had every year for a dollar a gallon.

DISCIPLINE, GRANDMOTHER TRIED

My Grandmother had three sons: Mark, Bill and Bob. Bill always minded, Mark and Bob would say no, get cranky, resist, etc.

One day she asked Bill to do something important and he said "I won't do it." She asked him several times to do it and he persisted with I won't do it. She threatened punishment and he stubbornly and defiantly said "I won't do it."

In frustration and anger my Grandmother took him down in the basement and gave him a swat with a piece of garden hose which went around him and the end came around and hit her on the leg. The hose didn't hurt Bill but the end really hurt and stung my Grandmother and at the same time made her want to laugh.

She hurriedly told him he could go now. Trying hard not to laugh in his presence. After he closed the door she sat down and laughed til she cried.

Discipline, Grandmother tried.

WOMEN TO WOMEN ADVICE

"Men can't be fixed"

GRANDMOTHER'S MEMORY

One of my happiest memories is riding double with my daughter Barby on our cowpony "Old Blue", bouncing along singing "Ragtime Cowboy Jo." Neither of us could carry a tune but we knew all the words and Blue seemed to enjoy it.

Grandmother Barbara Van Cleave
Louisville, KY

My granddaughter Timari reported in her paper that during
the Civil war, Connecticut
was very valuable in producing
arms and other body parts.

Mother Earth receives the love of Father Sun.
All life is dependent on that love.

When young, we were, really cool,
real busy, being, the fool.

Emotional excitement is often confused
with spiritual experience.

GRANDMOTHER

She has lived a long time
She is an old woman
She has endured the wars
Let her go.

She lived well in her time
Her body is old
She can't see much
She can't hear much
Let her go.

She can't eat
She can't walk
too weak is the body
Let her go.

Leave the life cycle alone
Let her continue her journey
Let her go.

We all have a turn
A time to go
Let her go.

We know, we accept
We are sad, we cry
We cry
We let her go.

EXPERIENCE

That which you receive in the greatest quantity,
shortly after, you really needed it.

TEENAGE REBEL

Teenage rebel with a cause.
No freedom, no choices
A life desired,
Smoking, drinking and drugging.
Pushing Death.
Studying & learning
Testing beyond the limits.
Testing reality.
What reality?
All reality.
Teenage rebel.

THE VALUE OF CHILDREN

When I was young
George had four small children.
   One day he said
"I wouldn't take a million
dollars for any one of my kids."
After a moments thought he added
"I wouldn't give a quarter for
another either."

POLITICIANS MOTTO

If at first you don't succeed
      try more craft & corruption
If you still don't succeed
      destroy the evidence

Too dumb to be a cowboy
Too smart to be a farmer.

OH WOMAN, OH WOMAN

Bloody Birth
Black & blue
Baby girl
laughin & cryin
playin & tryin
young girl
not so innocent
smarter than most
girl woman
    too soon
girl woman
    too long
chasin dreams
real & unreal
right & wrong
anger & passion
broken heart
cryin & cryin
pickin & singin
singin a song

Oh woman, oh woman

UNPREDICTABLE WOMEN

Been there and back
   more than once
      learned something
Woman
   are always
      unpredictable
You never can tell
   about women
And if you can
   you shouldn't

FEMALE GIFT

She pushed me
    back in time.
to the depths
    of origin

She pushed me
    forward
    beyond time.
Into the depths
    of mystery.

Once upon
    a time.

She loved me,
    almost.

DAMN WOMEN

I'd been workin on it
    for hours
Made some progress too
    It was together
One small problem
    It didn't work
I'd tried and tried
    and then some
Time and time again
    It still didn't work

She looked it all over
    broke the seal
Pulled out the instructions
    not only read `em
But she followed `em
    and to make matters
    even worse

It worked

Damn women

WOMEN FORMULA

My uncles
    success formula
      for women
  guaranteed
    great results.

My uncles
    success formula
      quite successful
        quite simple.

   - Just -

Treat queens
    like whores
  and
Treat whores
    like queens.

IT WAS

It was, she was
It was, in her eyes
    It was, in her talk
      It was, in her walk
A blind man, could see
    she was, a dreamer
      and a screamer
It was, she was

The old Lakota was wise. He knew that man's heart away
from nature becomes hard.
        Standing Bear

MEN

Men
fathering
Mother Earth
creating
safe places
for all life, nature.
Men nurturing
children
women
men
re-fathering
themselves.
Awakening
sleeping
spirits inside
becoming alive.
Protecting
fathering
all life.
Men.

BECOMING A MAN

"I don't wanna be little folk, I wanna be big folk" I said at age two. It wasn't OK to be little. At three, I was trying to smoke. It didn't work. I didn't know you were supposed to suck, not blow.

A few years later, with Dad's borrowed pipe, we were fishin and smokin down at the slough. We all got very sick. I knew I wasn't a man, but kept trying.

Later cigarettes and an older friend taught me the proper technique to inhale. At last I was a man.

Workin on the farm and ranch in the hay, dirt and chemicals and smokin heavy for ten years, resulted in me being one sick puppy, Winter flu, over celebratin New Years Eve and on January first, at age nineteen, too sick to smoke. I quit.

At last I was a man!

COWBOY FRIEND

Small New Mexico spread
   Horses, cows and goats
      Grew up too quick
Worked on the ranches
   Worked in town
      Worked all around
John was a purdy good hand
Drinkin and druggin
   Dancin and romancin
      Fightin and lyin
Trouble here, trouble there
   Red River showdown
      Main street
         4 against 20
Rodeo circuit
   Ridin them bulls
      Doin Fair
Close the bars
   Do a line
      Climb on a bull
Ridin free and fast
   Burnin up youth
      That couldn't last
Some said "It was the drugs"
Some said "It was the women"
Some said "It was lack of sleep"
Others said "It was bad luck"
Wrecked and broke
   Emergency room
      Gored by a bull
Quakin like a duck
   laughin and jokin
      Cowboy humor
Doctors cleanin, cuttin and stitchin
   Be quiet cowboy, quit moving
      If you want this slim chance
         to live at all
Lost his spleen
   part of his liver
      and stuff not keen

Heavy equipment operator
Overhaulin a truck
Trainin horses
Workin stock
Fixin fence
Raisin hell
Been in trouble, been in jail
John was a purdy good hand
In his late 20's
Lookin 50
Still carryin on
Cowboy code lived
Right and wrong
Somewhat twisted
Helpin people
Hurtin people
Mostly himself
John was a friend of mine
Workin up north
Last I heard
And I pray
He's doin fine
and stays up there

COWBOY/RANCHER DIFFERENCE

In the old days the difference between a cowboy and a rancher was: a cowboy spent his money rustling (mavericking) on frivolous things; a rancher spent his on land.

ORGANIC COWBOY

Work in BS all week
Talks BS Saturday night
Hears BS Sunday morning

WHY COWBOYS GET FIRED
FROM THEM CITY JOBS

Horses & cows, ropes & chutes
    Sweat & blood, yes blood
        Always a wreck, always an injury
            Workin cowboys always laugh

When they have a wreck
    workin livestock
        no matter the hurt & pain
            workin cowboys always laugh

Victim or observer
    wrecks & misfortunes
        no matter the damage
            workin cowboys always laugh

Cowboys always laugh at the time
    and again later
        tellin the story
            They laugh some more

In rural America
    on the farms and ranchers
        It's just part of the culture
            of singin the blues

Cowboys in the city
    Drivin them trucks
        Down any old road

Runnin them machines
    In any old factory
        Have wrecks too

Workin cowboys always laugh
    at the time and again later
Well - city folks certainly don't laugh
    At a time like this
        It ain't acceptable
            It damn sure ain't humorous
            and they get irritated
Which any county boy knows
    makes a cowboy
        laugh even harder
And then
    Them city folks
        they get irritated
            some more
And then - well

That's why cowboys get fired from them city jobs.

STARFISH COWBOY
OR
MAKIN A DIFFERENCE

The old cowboy was walkin the beach early in the mornin. The tide was out and lots of Starfish had been washed up on the sand. He was pickin 'em up and throwin 'em back in the ocean one at a time as he walked along.

A jogger saw him throw one in just before he got up to the cowboy. The old cowboy said "Howdy neighbor." The jogger stopped and told him, he'd just jogged 6 miles and there were thousands of Starfish washed up on the beach where he'd been. Besides there were thousands & thousands of miles of beach with millions & millions of Starfish washed up on them. The few you can throw back in wasn't going to make any difference.

The old cowboy just bent down picked up a Starfish and tossed it in the ocean and said "It made a difference to that one."

COWBOY TO RANCHER TO COWBOY

Ranchers own 'em
cows, calves and bulls
Cowboys work 'em
Sweat and blood
Ranchers worry more
keep books
Cowboys work harder
play harder
Cowboy to Rancher
years of dreamin
working and savin
Rancher to cowboy
one hand
5 card stud

OLD COWBOY

Anguish
the man
his face
the pain
his silence
His past
the scars.
A map
of mistakes.
Life lived
traveling
too fast.
Dust settling
in the wrinkles.

WHAT IS A COWBOY

Webster sez: One who tends or drives cattle. As usual the dictionary wasn't much help. It was then I noticed that Webster's was published in Massachusetts. That by itself explained quite a bit. Noah Webster probably had never been around any 100% cowboys. Here it is in the simplest terms that even someone back east can understand.
A cowboy is:
10% cow
10% boy
80% bullshit
100% cowboy

In growing old, one grows more foolish and wise.

CONNECTING STORIES

Old cowboys
Tellin stories
About the past
of youth
Raisin hell
Good times
and bad
About life
and livin
and dreamin
The stories
Selective memories
Growin and flowin
Appearin & disappearin
Old men
Always connectin
In the stories.

RELATIVELY POOR OLD COWBOY

The old cowboy had worked on area ranches all his life. He was a good hand willin and able to do the work of a cowboy.

He didn't like to be told how to do anything. Shortly after being supervised he'd quit and move on. He had the bare minimum of clothes & possessions.

A young feller asked the old cowboy what he had to show for a lifetime of hard work? He reply "I ain't got nuttin but a bunch of relatives so I'm relatively poor."

TALK

Talk is not cheap
and money talks

EARLY COWBOY ROMANTIC IMAGE

When my grandmother's father was visitin with his sister from eastern Colorado, he told her about the new glorified romantic eastern image of the cowboys.

She said "Sh---oot, (that ain't what she really said) Sh--oot, cowboys ain't nuthin but farm hands with big hats.

INTERSTATE TRUCK STOP COWBOY

The Southeast corner of the ranch was across from the interstate truck stop.

About noon this old cowboy rode up to the corner, pulled off his boots, put on a pair of tennis shoes. He then proceeded to loosen the cinch and tie his horse to the fence, climbed thru, walked across to the truck stop cafe.

A retired couple in the RV observed all this and were discussing with each other as to why on earth would a real cowboy take off his boots, put on tennis shoes to eat lunch at a truck stop. They couldn't figure it out and decided to ask him when he came out.

When stopped and asked why he took off his boots & put on tennis shoes to have lunch at the truck stop the old cowboy replied "I sure didn't want them folks in there to think I was a truck driver."

SENSITIVE COWBOY

He asked his girlfriend upon her return from
the restroom if everything had come out OK.

TROUBLED

We're troubled some by what's
happening around us
We're troubled more by what's
happening inside us

WRONG

Yes, he knew it was wrong.
No, he didn't stop, he went ahead,
Because, he really wanted,
To belong.

EQUALLY EFFECTIVE
PREVENTION & CURE TREATMENT

Banging ones head against the wall to prevent
headaches works just as well as banging one
head against the wall to cure headaches.

YOUR CHOICE

The Great Spirit casts light on your spiritual path.
We pray that you may see it, follow it, live it &
love your spiritual path.

FAMOUS INDIAN

More famous
    than
the father of
    our country
more famous
    than Jesus
more famous
    than any
person living
    or dead.

Famous Indian
    most famous
        signs everywhere.

His name
    Falling Rock

NATIVE MISSIONARIES

Native American Missionaries
Great idea
too late in asking

What could have been
    Native American
        medicine men
            medicine women
    Missionaries
Native American Missionaries
    Teaching Europeans
        To love, share & respect
            Mother Earth
            all life
        History reversed

Native American Missionaries
    Great idea
        Too late in asking

Missionaries

TALKIN NICE

More than
talkin nice
Apache trick
European Invasion
Restless & Ruthless
talkin nice
Surveyors surveyin
talkin nice
Bureaucrats perkin
Treaties forced
Treaties ignored
Manifest destiny
Greedy ones
Iron hearts
talkin nice
Apache trick
more than
talkin nice
Apache a foot
runnin down
Horseback enemy
Horse a dyin
closin in
Enemy killed
Horse riden
another 20 miles
Apache trick
More than
talkin nice
Apache trick

1830 ON INDIANS
by one white man, who knew

I love a people, who have always made me welcome, to the best they had --- who are honest without laws --- who never take the name of God in vain --- who worship God without a bible --- and I believe God loves them too.
George Catlin, Artist 1830

NAVAHO MESSAGE TO THE MOON

Back in 1966 the Apollo team was on the Navaho reservation where the terrain is similar to the moon. There were trucks, heavy equipment computers, engineers, scientists and lots of other personnel around 2 astronauts in full space gear walking over the rock formations.

Across the valley was an old Navaho & his young grandson watching over a herd of sheep and the Apollo team. Two Apollo executives drove over and walked up the hill and explained that they were preparing to go to the moon. The grandson spoke to his grandfather in Navaho explaining what the executives had told him in English. The old man excitedly asked if he could send a message with them to the moon in Navaho.

The executives had a quick conference and radioed for a tape recorder. After the old grandfather recorded the message they asked the grandson to translate it for them. He refused, and couldn't be budged.

The evening they went into the city for dinner. They asked several Navahos to translate the message but they all stoically refused. After dinner they found a half drunk wino who quickly took the $10 offered and translated the message "Beware, these palefaces come to take your land."

Tell them how we loved all that was beautiful.
American Indian

CRAZY WHITE MAN

Crazy white man
Offered the old Indian
beautiful beads
blankets & things

Crazy white man
wanted land
old Indian
knew you can't
buy, sell or trade
Mother Earth.

More beautiful beads
old Indian
threw in
the Brooklyn Bridge
crazy white man

Many year later
Crazy white man
Shuffling papers
still don't know
you can't
buy, sell or trade
Mother Earth

Crazy white man

HITLER AND THE AMERICAN INDIANS

What Hitler did to the Jews
was about the same
as they did
to the American Indians.

Indulgences are straying from your spiritual path.

RESERVATION PREACHER

Fat and soft
Preaching lies
Begging money

Arrogant and proud
of his Indian name
Walking Eagle

Reservation preacher
didn't know
the meaning

Walking Eagle
too full of shit
to fly.

BUFFALO TEARS

Buffalo tears
    Stretched
Coast to coast
    Four strands
Bible belt
    Barbed, pointed
and sharp.

Buffalo tears
    Silently crying.

In memory
    of a better day

Before the invasion

Buffalo tears

CAYUSE

Northwest
thousands of years
Cayuse Indians.
From the south
Spanish horses
Cayuse progress.
Hudson Bay Company
Cayuse trappers
Anglo progress.
Cayuse horses
many buyers
immigrants and settlers.
Cayuse Indians
kept the best
traded the rest.
Cayuse horses
bad habits, dispositions
always a problem.
Hudson Bay Company
selling cattle
Cayuse ranchers.
Land, cattle & horses
Cayuse Indians
Cayuse cowboys.
Insatiable greed
Army troops
Cayuse prisons.
Cayuse Indians
Cayuse cowboys
mostly forgotten.
Cayuse horses
bad habits, dispositions
always a problem.
Cayuse horses
here, there and everywhere
always a problem.

Always remembered.

Cayuse.

INDIAN LAMENT

From the East
  The arrival
    White eyes

Goddamies
  Bringing Christianity
    their true God

That's when
  It began
    Our true misery

White diseases
  Old to them
    New to us

The stench
  of illness
    and death

True suffering
  Young and old
    Our true misery

Buffalo gone
  Sad replacement
    Slow elk

Army bullets
  Reservation prisons
    Barbed wire

Paradise lost
  Whiskey soaked
    Our true misery

Indian Lament

INDIAN NICKNAMES

Mirror reflection, Indian nicknames
European invaders, Indian perceptions
Palefaces, Indian nickname
Hollywood popular, white man profitable
Indian nickname, Goddamies
Mirror reflection, favorite word
Sona Bitchie, Indian perception
White man's most famous Saint
European invaders, Iron Hearts
Indian perception, cuts to the bone
Indian nickname, greedy ones
gets right to the point, truth reflected
Loco ones, those who do everything backwards
Indian humor, Indian perception
Indian nicknames.

INDIANS COULDN'T BELIEVE

Indians couldn't believe
insatiable greed
heaven or hell
insanity
creating hell
from heaven
on Earth - our Mother.
Takers, insanity
never giving
always reaching
for more.
Something new
never enough
insanity.
Indians couldn't believe,
insatiable greed,
heaven or hell.

NO WAY, INDIAN

Freedom of religion
    Freedom from religion
no way, Indian.

Government sponsored
    Christian missionaries
Conquer and convert

Bill of rights
    religious freedom
no way, Indian
    1978
new law, new treaty
American Indian
Religious Freedom act
    Hoorah - Hoorah
        1978

Native American church
    four sacred sacraments
        cedar & sage
        tobacco & peyote

Peyote! -Peyote!
    war on drugs
new law, new treaty
    religious freedom
no way, Indian.

One more
    broken treaty
How many?
376 - 100% broken

Freedom of religion
Freedom from religion
no way, Indian

CHARLEY

Charley was a friend of mine
always put it back
Red, white or black
Raised a Mormon
St John's graduate
Charley weren't no moron
Midnight plumber
Drove the bus
Taught the classes
Pockets & bag full
Charley always had it
School was never dull
Gently guiding
always questioning
Charley's way
made our day
Charley was a teacher
helper and a leader
never was a preacher
When it got tough
He wasn't gruff
Charley knew
Love was glue
There's been some gore
Cheez Charley, more cheez
the mouse is gonna roar
Midnight plumber
Drove the bus
Taught the classes
Charley did it all
Until his final call.
Charley was a friend of mine.

Our songs are part of nature, life.
American Indian

NAVAJO MAN

Not young
   not old
      coal miner.

Navajo man
   still alive
      followed
         white man's
            religion
Spirit weakened
   nearly lost
Spirit calling
   Navajo man
     listening
   and   dreaming

Navajo Man

The pulse of Mother Earth
slows our own in a calming way.

We may quarrel with men about things
on earth, but we never quarrel
about the Great Spirit.
Chief Joseph

The River flows around the bend
and in a moment we grow old.

SOMETHING DEEPER

Cheyenne woman
beautiful
Her picture
in my mind
A feeling
in my heart
and something deeper.

N train
San Francisco
Long ago
we never
Touched
Yet something
deeper
Than love
or lust
Still remains
from
Long ago

Cheyenne Woman

Something Deeper.

ADAM AND EVE

You all know the story of Adam and Eve. What you probably don't know is that when Adam took the bite out of the apple he looked off in the distance and saw an Indian working in his field.

Adam was of course surprised, he choked on the apple, it stuck in his throat. And that is why white people have Adam's apples.

APPLIED COMMON SENSE

The unwritten ranch rule regardin gates is leave 'em like you find 'em.

Translated for you complicated city folks: if you drive up to a closed gate, you get out and open it, drive thru, get out and close it. If you drive up to an open gate you simply drive on thru and leave it open. Sounds like simple common sense, and it is, and isn't.

Any ranch person can tell you horror stories where this simple rule was ignored resulting in bulls gettin in with heifers, separated herds gettin mixed as closed gates were left open, cattle dyin, gettin tangled up in fences trying to get to water when an open gate was closed, etc., etc.

When I was young and visited city relatives with indoor plumbing, I naturally applied the common sense ranch gate rule to the toilet seat and lid. Leave 'em like you find 'em. There was no complaints except mine about the unusual sensation of cold water splashing my tender hind quarters.

More recently there was a big thing (probably started by feminists) about men leaving the toilet seats up instead of down. The controversy raged and got full coverage by TV, radio, newspapers. The talk shows had a field day interviewing famous people on the toilet seat subject.

Us rural people had the applied common sense not to get involved in this foolishness of city folks.

CITY SLICK - COUNTRY REDNECK

New cars
  double garage
    city slick
Old trucks
  all around
    country redneck
Manicured lawn
  no livestock
    fresh paint
      city slick
Weeds standin tall
  Livestock & sign
    fresh pies & muffins
      country redneck
Flush toilets
  showers every day
    mornin & nite
      city slick
Old outhouse
  Saturday bath
    livestock perfume
      country redneck
Vacuum cleaner
  new dishes
    olive oil
      city slick
Shovel & a broom
  old black skillet
    bacon grease
      country redneck
Chandelier
  dimmer switch
    electronic surveillance
      city slick
Coleman lantern
  wood matches
    hound dogs
      country redneck
City slick
  Country redneck

THE BARN & THE MAILBOX
or
Damn City Slicker

For sixty years
    and then some
The old rancher
    walked to the barn
Saddled a horse
    rode down
       and got the mail

A visitor
    this city slicker
       one day
Observed
    this long-standin
       ritual
This city slicker
    he figured out
       it was
          further
To the barn
    than to the mailbox

Damn City Slicker

CONVERSATION WITH GOD

My friend Barbara Ann was talking with God a while back and asked her "What can you tell me about the churches and religions of the world today?" She answered "They're doing about the same today as they have for 10,000 years: Everything possible to prevent anyone from having a spiritual experience."

BARBARA ANN

Barbara Ann once said
"Over 95% of what we do is unnecessary."

LIFE, DIDN'T THEY TELL YOU?

I'm a country boy
didn't they tell you?

I've been east
north, west
and south.
I've been to Phoenix
Tucson, too
NYC, Boston
Houston, Austin
Atlanta, Nashville

I've been all around

Didn't they tell you
about life?

Let me tell you
about life.

It's kinda like
running barefoot
down a gravel road.

BLUE EYES

Your eyes so blue, can't be true
I know that you know
My heart's, with you - and
It's true, eyes so blue
Can't be true
It's been, a long time
And you're still, on my mind
We're so, far apart - yet
Heart to heart
And I know, that you know
Eyes so blue, can't be true
Blue Eyes

DEVOTED PEOPLE

Devoted to money
Devoted to hype
Devoted to scientific progress
Devoted to entertainment
Devoted to lifesyles dictated by advertising
Devoted to technology
Devoted to material gadgets
Devoted to automobiles
Devoted to conveniences
Devoted to forgetting the Spiritual

SUGGESTED CHANGES

Change your resentments into acceptance
Change your anger into love
Change your fear into hope

SURGEONS: SURGERY OPPORTUNITY

Personality transplants.

His knife was so dull, had to heat it up some to cut butter.

Ordinary human love is capable of raising man
to the experience of real love.
Hakin Jami, Sufi

Mules are smarter than horses.
Mules are more sure footed than horses.

ANGEL

Angel
Angel from hell
Living on
The razors edge.

Angel
An axe to grind
A walk to walk
Screaming silently
Midnight Moon

Angel
Emotional bleeding
Still burning
Angel from hell
Always a fee
Nothing for free
Angel, impossible to train
And I forgot her name
Angel from hell

Angel

THE STORYTELLER

Children, crowding closer to hear
The Storyteller
   Stories from
Meditation, magic & mystery
   Stories from
Feeling, remembering & living
The Storyteller
Melting the past
   into the present & future
The pain
   moaning & crying
The joy
   smiling & laughing
Celebrating life
   children crowding closer to hear
The Storyteller

MORE IMPORTANT THAN
NEBRASKA FOOTBALL

Jake Vohland was a plumber, not like the ones today. His attitude and prices were a bit different too. Jake's plumbing definitely wouldn't of passed any codes though it worked and lasted a long time. He used galvanized pipe and would run it right up to the outlet using few fittings, bending the pipe to fit. Jake also fixed a lot of windmills.

One fall, Jake was taking his grandson to see a football game in Lincoln. They left at 5:00 in the morning and were a little over halfway there when Jake noticed a herd of thirsty cattle near the road around a tank and windmill. He stopped to check, the tank was dry and the windmill wasn't pumping any water. This was quite a ways from home and he had no idea whose place it was or whose cattle they were. Jake turned the car around and they went back home and got his old panel truck with plumbing tools and supplies and came back and fixed the windmill.

More important than Nebraska football.

ON RICHES

We do not want riches.
We want peace, and love.
Red Cloud 1870

SIN

An Ancient archery term, meaning, off the mark. Applied to your spiritual path, sin means, your heart's not in it.

GUEST POET

Truth or Consequences
 Hot Springs Middle School
 Friday afternoon
Writing class
 7th, 8th & 9th graders
 Rows of students
Guest poet, yours truly
 Talking & reading
 Observing youth
Rows of students
 Mostly not listening
 Minds already set
Asking questions
 To please the teacher
 Hoping for a better grade
Guest poet scattering seeds
 On the wind of words
 Mostly lost & wasted
Yet--a few seeds planted
 In fertile young minds
 For the future
 Guest Poet

LIMITED RIGHTS

Our rights are limited to where another's begin.

EVERYTHING

Attitude is everything.

BEAUTY

She was more than beautiful
I'm grateful for the love and lust
Ran the course & couldn't last
and yes, I'm healin fast
Laying back on Mother Earth
Looking up at Father sky
thru the beauty of a tree
that was standin high
Hugged and kissed that tree
In the mountains of New Mexico
Knowin I was more than free
while baskin in all the mystery
My nose deep in the bark
Breathin in the sweetness
Disappearin in the ponderosa pine
Realizin I hadn't been kind
She was more than beautiful
I'm grateful for the love and lust
Ran the course and couldn't last
And yes, I'm healing fast

THE MOON

Old George Maul told about one time his neighbor, Art asked him & Jim to help gather his cows on Wednesday so they could wean the calves. Jim said he couldn't do it on Wednesday but would be glad to help toward the end of the week. Art kinda sheepishly said "no we gotta do the weanin on Wednesday while the moon is right."

Jim said "Art, I know you're purdy smart, surely you don't believe in that silly superstition about weanin with the moon, do you?"

Art replied "of course not, I don't believe in such foolish superstitions as that, but them dumb cows & calves do."

CATHOLIC JUMP

Roger died
Catholic friend
Funeral and burial
Catholic priest $1,000

Steady progress
From hell
to purgatory
Catholic priest $1,000

Six months
Praying and fussing
Leaving purgatory
Catholic priest $1,000

So close
Yet so far
working hard
Catholic priest $1,000

Money all gone
Big parish
Catholic priest
many duties
My Catholic friend
Roger, on his own
Jumped into heaven
Catholic Jump

ON CREATION

We were contented to let things remain as the Great Spirit
made them.
Chief Joseph 1873

DOCTOR GREASEMONKEY

Car Doctor
    angry and resentful
        making less
    than
        people doctors

Doctor Greasemonkey
    tired of
        customer complaints
    Detroit iron
        imports
    lower pay
        went to school too
    angry and resentful
        car doctor
Doctor Greasemonkey.

FAST ICE - SLOW LADY

Beautiful lady
    named Linda
        - Just -
wild enough
    crazy enough
        to be interesting
Slow lady - Fast ice

She always filled the
ice cube trays with
steaming hot water, swearing that

Hot water
    freezes faster
        than cold water

Fast Ice - Slow Lady

DOCTORS

State licensed
to practice
members AMA

Expensive equipment
Expensive lifestyle
Expensive insurance

Malpractice
High risk
Danger
Drugs
Doctors
State licensed
to practice
Doctors
just practicing
DANGER
just practicing

DEBRA

Spirits calm
Radiating
Power
Magic
Mystery
Life
Eyes and smiles
Communication
Laughter & sharing
Exciting
Playful
Comforting
Old souls
Celebrating
the moment
Forever
Timeless
Then and now.
Debra

HERO

Abused child
Jewish grandfather
Crazy Aunt, in house
Insanity denied.

Incest, failed student
dreaming & brooding
failed artist
failed marriages

Political peach
grown up
abundant drugs
experimental doctors
sexual deviant

Doors opening
opportunities seized
climbing fast
power gained
abounding illusions

Boy scouts
new uniforms
new name
new symbol
stolen & reversed

Patriotism, nationalism
super race
super effort
super power

Hero bound
Hitler
third Reich
S S troops
war machine

You know
the rest
of the story.

GOD MADE RANCHERS

Yes, I see your bumper sticker
    God made ranchers
I've been told
    God made Earth
    Sun & stars
    Water & trees
    Plants & mountains
    Animals & birds
And God made everything
    I've been told
      So
Perhaps God made
    Ranchers too
Who made cowboys?
Who made God?
    Well
She ain't sayin
    no one
wants to talk
    about
their mistakes.

GARRET AND ELLA MAE

Our neighbor
    Garret Jurgens
Told me
    that when
They were young
    they would fight
Just so
    They could
make up.

I'm dangerous, I think.

GOOD OLD REBEL

Served with Robert E. Lee
   three years about
Got wounded in four places
   starved at point lookout
Caught the rheumatism
   campin out in the snow
Killed a sight 0 Yankees
   wished I'd ah killed som mo
For I'm a good old rebel
   that's what I am
And for the land O freedom
   Ah don't care a damn
Ah'm glad I fought agin her
   I only wish we'd won
Ah don't ask no pardons
   for anything I've done
Ah hates the constitution
   the great Republic too
Ah hates the mighty Eagle
   and the uniform of blue
Ah hates the glorious banner
   and all their flags & fuss
Them lyin, thievin Yankees
   ah hates 'em wuss & wuss
All won't be reconstructed
   I'm better now then them
For those dirty carpetbaggers
   Ah don't give a damn
So I'm off to the border
   as soon as I can go
I'll get me a gun
   and leave for old Mexico

For Ah'm a good old rebel
    that's what Ah am
And for the land of freedom
    Ah don't care a damn
Ah'm glad I fought against her
    I only wish we'd won
and Ah don't ask no pardon
    for anything I've done.

by Innes Randalph

Good old Rebel in World War I
Born in North Carolina
Raised in Tennessee
Worked like hell in Georgia
Died in Germany

THE GODS LAUGH

The gods are laughing
nonstop, out of control
rolling & falling

The Gods have been, are
and will forever....

Laugh at their own joke
    PEOPLE

INDIAN PRAYER

Jesus, please protect me from your followers.

FRENCHIE

Bosque Mountains, age eleven, farmed out.
Ranch hand, room & board, dollar a month.
Child's pay, man's work.

Montana Mountains, contract sheepherder
9 months, alone, burro, sheep.

Oregon coast, logger, responsible,
promoted, foreman, Swedish crew.

California milker, 40 cows, twice daily,
every day, by hand.
Money earned, Money saved.

New Mexico, Agua Fria, working harder,
his place, his cows.
Sunshine Dairy.

Milk cows, feed 'em, milk 'em, doctor 'em too.
He knew, all the tricks, a lifetime of learning
& makin do.

Heavy accent. Huge hands, old & strong.
Teeth gone, a snag or two.
Milk, dollar, a gallon.

A story every time. Finger prop,
Hardness of youth, Softness of age.
Frenchie laughed, about it all.
The pain, joy, struggles of life.
He survived, his family, the hardships, the years,
hard work, survived the depression,
and cut throat competition.

Never married, never in the army, old & failing,
Sargent nearly got him.

They called, him Frenchie. His name was,
Barnard Parachu.

He was, a friend, of mine.

LARRY'S WEDDING

I remember Larry's first date. I don't remember who I was with but he was with Margie, that's not the girl he's marrying. Margie was slim and sweet with long blond hair. She was flat chested, I don't think Larry minded that as he kept trying! It just didn't work out for them. It didn't work out for me either. I wasn't to be married till August of 1958, of course I didn't know that then. It was very important to get married back in those days.

June, 1956, my friend Larry was getting married. He had become a Catholic! Larry wanted me to be the best man but I wasn't Catholic and the priest insisted on a Catholic. Hell, I wasn't even a Christian, never baptized, the priest didn't know all this so I was an usher.

Saturday morning, Larry and Mary Ann were getting married. He wasn't much on drinking back in those days, no hangover, just hungry. The Catholic rule was, he couldn't eat till after the wedding. Well Wilbur & I had drank his share and more than our share, we were definitely hungover, sick for sure.

Alcohol and cigarettes were the only drugs around then and not even thought of as drugs, coffee was a social drink and a cure for too much alcohol. In our case it hadn't helped.

It was a full blown, formal, full service Catholic wedding and everyone was nervous as hell anyhow. Those who knew the groom's stag party resulted in the ushers (Wilber & me) being in the terrible shape we were in, were even more nervous.

It all went fairly smooth and everyone was seated with the ceremony being all sanctified and all. The time came when us men in the wedding party stood up from the pew we were sitting in to walk up and join the bride and groom, best man and bridesmaid, and of course the priest. Wilbur was at the end of the pew and when he stepped out into the aisle he tripped on the kneeling rail and landed on his face in the middle of the aisle.

Everyone knew he wasn't Catholic!

THE FIRST ARTIST

The first artist
was a man
pissing
in the snow

JANE

After the introduction
we tried, to talk
no way
no one knew
what happened

Reality suspended
Spiritual magic
uncontrollable.

Something like
a melt down
of our souls

In that moment
real life
didn't exist

Yet more real
than the
pleasure & pain
that followed

Jane

JOSEPH

Late one night after dinner visiting with guests in the parlor my
great-grandfather Joseph announced "let's go to bed so these
nice people can go home."

JACK PRELUTSKY POETRY FESTIVAL

Jack Prelutsky
  Poetry Festival
    Kearney Library

Jack Prelutsky will read
  Backwards & forewards
    In a circle

I think My newspaper is crazy
  Like an apprentice Witch
    On Monday's Troll

No Jack
  No Sun
    Some ice
      Some fun

Jack ain't crabby
  Just ain't comin
    Glad we got Abby
      Talkin & readin

Two boys
  Too quiet
    Two girls
      Two gigglin

Some New Kids
  On the block
    Running upstairs
      Running downstairs

Something Big
  Has been here
    Like that pig
      Over there
Eating a pizza
  The size of
    The sun

At the Jack Prelutsky
  Poetry Festival
    Kearney Library

JUST ANOTHER LOVER

Just another lover
        except
This time
        you're
            afraid
        to admit
It is more
        than
Just another lover.

INSTANT FORGIVENESS

She stepped
        out of nowhere

Quick on the brakes
        Cussin & swearin
She looked
        at me
            and smiled
Beautiful lady
Instant forgiveness

MIKES

Her name was Mike
Mike married a friend
        of mine
His name was Mike
they had a baby
and they named him
        Mike

Mike & Mike & Mike

HONEY

She called me honey
   She spent
      my money

Oh what a treat
   Love so sweet

She called me honey
   She spent
      my money

Honey

MARTIN

He was alive
strong, handy
   and gentle
Handsome In
   a way
Reckless and wild

Loved life
   woman
      Divorced

Wild and Free

Motorcycle
   no insurance
   no plates
   no lights

Midnight ride
   Martin
He was alive.

PAST WIFE, PAST LIFE

Too young
    to be bad
Too old
    to be good
Legalized sex
    marriage.
Children
    too young
Too busy
    too crazy
Too many
    changes
Too late
    in coming
Divorce
    legalized pain
A lifetime
    of anger
outran
    catching up fast.
I remembered
    I didn't love you, enough
I forgot
    I liked you, a lot
Once upon a time
    a long time ago
Past life
    past wife.

SPANISH OR MEXICAN?

I was helping Larry Herrera install some gas lines when someone asked if he was Spanish or Mexican, he replied "Well I make less than $15,000 a year so I'm a Mexican."

OLD CULT - SLOW CULT

Virgin Mary
    waiting patiently

Women waiting
    years & years

The trinity
    all male
Virgin Mary
Held back
    waiting & waiting

Old dogma

1958, Finally
Virgin Mary
Placed in heaven
    by the
Catholic Church

Old Cult - slow cult

SMILE

The old man
    smiled and
        the years
    melted away

    s m i l e

Optimist dealing with reality.
Pessimist?

NIKKI

You've always been more than kind
　　and your poem's been on my mind
　　　　your anger caught me by surprise
　　　　　about men lustin after you

It's all kinda close to home
　　yet far away as Rome
　　　　cause I've lusted too
　　　　　　and your poem's been on my mind

I've hugged and kissed a tree
　　I've been caged and I've been free
　　　　I've ran to and from
　　　　　Beauty, love and lust

I don't have the answers
　　for you or anyone
　　　　but men will continue to
　　　　　To lust after you

And Nikki your poem's
　　been on my mind.

WILLOW

Willow sent me a card and 2 very small
　　beautiful hummingbird feathers.

The message:
Our hearts cry for what we have lost.
Our spirit laughs in joy
　　for what we have gained.

Extinct is probably forever.

SON-IN-LAW

Pretty boy
born a ladies man
wonderful dancer
my daughter married him
tall, blond and handsome.

Darker skin, black hair
his mother, part Indian
he was part crazy

#1 salesman in the USA
selling vacuums and himself
Living high, new house
new Cadillacs, two daughters.

Abusive, irresponsible
drinkin, drugin and workin
woman chasin, too much like me
when I was younger
Same thing, only different
Except
He followed a crazy Preacher
born again Cocaine Christian

Pretty boy
born a ladies man
wonderful dancer
my daughter married him
tall, blond and handsome

Moved in
with another woman.

One too many
Divorce
Ex Son-In-Law

STYLE AND MARRIAGE, ALMOST

My Grandmother's
mother almost
married a man
named Hart.

The high style
at that time
was narrow
shoes that is.

His surgery
outer toes
surgically removed
narrow shoes
stylish for sure.

Romance ended
she married
a man
named Bolin
wide feet.

No style.

OLD MAN

When my oldest son was three, he called my Dad the old man. We, of course, reprimanded him on the spot and told him not to call his grandfather the old man.

My son got that look on his face and was silent for a few moments and then replied "Well, he still looks like an old man to me."

Honor Mother Earth.

TERESA

New love
   old love.
When did
   we meet?
Oh yes
   now
   I remember.
It was
   10,000 years ago.
We loved
   each other
   then
   and
We love
   each other
   now.
Old love
   new love.

YOU MIGHT BE A REDNECK ...

if you were ever called Bubba.
if you take your dog to work with you.
if you ride your horse to work.
if you ate lunch at the bait shop.
if you wear new cowboy boots while
   your wife goes barefoot.
if your wife has a double first name.
if you move to a city and the welcoming
   committee doesn't come to visit you.
if both your cars are old pickups.
if you ate duck or lizard for dinner.

Sheep ruled by pigs.

TEACHER

Mary Anderson, common name
Mary Elizabeth Anderson, not so common
Mary Elizabeth Anderson
   teacher and more

Sharp as a tack, my dad would say
Strong heart, Grey Antelope would say
Not young, not old
   probably never will be
     I'd say

Writing class, successful writer
Educated by the school of hard knocks
preserving thru experience and rejects
Hard work and discipline
paying off, sharing success
   with others.

Teacher

Mary Elizabeth Anderson

SANTA DID THE BEST HE COULD

Old man Cook said that when he was about 12, a young boy in the neighborhood wanted a pony for Christmas. His family was very poor and couldn't afford one.

On Christmas morning the boy found in his Christmas stocking two small horse turds and a note from Santa saying, sorry the pony got away.

Those claiming God is on their side
are dangerous as hell.

TYPICAL FARMER

November 4th, 1997
Depressed and repressed
Corn harvest
Half done
Before the big wind
After the rain
Before the big snow
Fightin the mud
Fightin the snow
Fightin the ice
Fightin the combine
Buildup & freezeups
Breakdowns
Stuff ain't built
for what we're
puttin it thru
Fightin the banker
Fightin the landlord
Fightin the neighbor's bull
Fightin the kids
Fightin the wife
She just ain't built
for what we're
putting her thru
Overdone folks
overdose
Depressed and repressed
November 4th 1997
Typical Farmer

GO GETTER

When the old rancher was asked what kind of a man his new son-in-law was he replied "He's a go getter. My daughter works at the plant in town and at 5:00 every day he goes and gets her."

THANKSGIVING & MANIFEST DESTINY

Pilgrims... Plymouth Rock... 1620... Pilgrims starving.. Indians fed 'em... Saved their asses.. Big Feast with love.. Thanksgiving.

Grateful Pilgrims never forgot. Paid back them Indians. Black Robes giving beads & cloth, teaching Christianity with bibles, bullets and booze.

Grateful Pilgrims never forgot, manifest destiny, obviously inevitable and apparent, even desirable they say. Progress... good for the economy.

Grateful Pilgrims never forgot, Manifest Destiny... Christian Soldiers marching as to war. European conquerors.. Iron Hearts.. Killing everything. Spreading disease, death & destruction through out Indian Paradise.

Grateful Pilgrims never forgot, still celebrate thanksgiving, big feast.. no Indians.

OLD TIME BARBERSHOP

Barber post; Red, white & blue.
One price - cheap. Haircut
Guarantee: guaranteed to be
shorter than when you came in.

CANCER CELLS

An example of growth for growth's sake,
and they even look like a city.

Humans aren't the only species on Earth,
they just act like it.

YUPPIES NOT HIPPIES

Mansion on the hill
    condo in Vail
Yuppies
    not hippies
Red brick madhouse
    cocaine therapy
Hot wired
    and juiced
Yuppies
    not hippies
Hit by
    the Mack truck
of unreal reality
Heterosexual dollars
    copulating
not so freely.

Yuppies
  not
     hippies

SOUND MAN

My Dad, Mark Randall, ran the projector for the silent films at the first movie theatre in Gibbon, Nebraska when he was a teenager. Being mechanically inclined he did a good job.

When talkies first came out the sound was on a big flat record. The record player was totally separate from the projector and had a control to speed it up or slow it down. Dad would start them both up at the same time and then continually adjust the speed on the record to keep the sound synchronized with the movie. He did alright on the dialogue and action parts of the movie but would always get lost when they did a song and be off for awhile after the song finished.

His very low musical ability proved a disaster on showing the first musical and Dad quit shortly after that. Ex sound man.

REAL PEOPLE

Artists, musicians, singers
writers, poets and shamans
are real people, almost.

We just cry more
    suffer more
We just laugh more
    feel more
We just love more.

Always searching in
    the mystery
    the magic
    in you, others
    and in ourselves.

Artists, musicians, singers
writers, poets and shamans
We're real people.

Almost!

GEORGE BAILEY SR.

George Bailey Sr.
    beat the IRS.
Smart enough
    didn't need
        an attorney.
George Bailey
    no education
        no bank
            no records.
On trial
    smart enough
        to act
            dumb enough.
Cash in hand.
George Bailey Sr.
    beat the IRS.

EXPERT COUNTER

The count
   Never questioned
      Expert counter
Bowlegged and crippled
   Stiff and slow
      Old cowboy
Standin on the rail
   At the gate
      Eyes alert and quick
Dust cloud
   Stampedin by
      Bawlin, bellerin & crowdin
Mixed herd
   Cows, calves and bulls
      All sizes and colors
The count
   Never questioned
      Expert counter
Buyer and seller
   Money exchanged
      Movin on
Greenhorn observer
   Stampeding herd
      NY city baffled
Asked the old cowboy
   How could anyone
      Possibly count 'em
He replied-Easy-
   Just count the feet
      Divide by 4
The count
   Never questioned
      Expert Counter.

AGAIN

I put my ear
　　to the sound
　　　　of her life

I put my nose
　　into the window
　　　　of her life

My eyes
　　wide open
　　　　beauty blinded

I didn't see
　　a damn thing
　　　　until

It was
　　too late

Again

BRONCO FACED COW

Bronco faced
　　wayward cow
Fence crawler
　　over, under
　　around and thru
She always knew
　　the grass
　　　　was greener
　　　　　　and better
Over there
　　wanderin wayward

Bronco Faced Cow

WINO

Swimming in the Wine
Too many years
Yesterday and tomorrow
Already lost
In the prison
of alcoholism
Empty bottle
Full as a tick
Legs melting away
Barely able
to fall down
and roll
into nowhere
Alcohol wings
collapsing in flight
Thru the concrete
decomposing into monsters
Free fall
into Hell
Wino

Republican government: Man exploits Man
Democratic government: Just reversed

If you want a country run by religion,
move to Iran.

Sorry I missed church, I've been busy
practicing witchcraft and becoming a lesbian.

SPRING CALVIN

Early mornin knock on the door. Dad, I'm gonna need some help pullin a calf.

I put on my boots, hat and coat. The old truck was runnin and warm. We headed out across the pastures. My youngest son Robert drivin and talkin, gravely concerned and excited.

"That fence crawlin bronco-faced cow is calvin and in bad trouble. I don't know how the hell she got there but she's standin on her head upside down in a steep washout with her feet in the air just kickin and bawlin and to make matters even worse the calf is comin ass backwards."

We drove to the washout and stopped. It was empty, only a wet spot of evidence near the top. My son said "I can't believe she's gone, dead yes, but not gone."

We drove over the hill and there standin was a new born calf being licked by that bronco faced cow.

The moral of this true story is: any cow smart enough to stand on her head, sure don't need no help havin a calf.

END OF THE LINE

Red
    we called her.
A milk cow
    reddish in color.
Best milk cow
    in the county.
    Easiest milker, too.
I remember
    four years old
    learning to milk.
Red
    big & scary.
    She never moved.
    Calm & steady.
Dad said
    "We're going
    to save her heifer
    calves for the herd."
He always said
    "50-50 chance
    for a female
    every time."
18 calves
    6 sets twins
    5 singles
    all male.
She died calving
    another male.
    End of the line.

COW PROOF GATE

That's what the advertisement said. It was built of heavy steel tubing and was 7 feet tall with heavy hinges and a fast latch so you could just slam the gate shut. We hung it on the entrance to the alley going to the squeeze chute for workin cows. The last gate was made of 2 X 8's bolted together with double cross braces. A big upset ole cow had made it into kindlin wood the last time we worked cattle.

Everything was workin real good. George & I would drive a few cows in the alley & swing this new gate shut behind them. A couple of rank cows had already tested it and I'd said to George "This gate is the best thing we've gotten since the squeeze chute." We agreed it was cow proof, strong & heavy, well designed and being 7' tall no cow could get thru it.

Later, about mid afternoon a young, wild black Angus cow went crazy in the alley after the gate was shut. She came chargin back at me & the gate on a dead run blowin snot and her eyes all glazed over. Well I forgot the gate was cow proof and took a few quick steps backwards. She hit the gate with a crash and it held, but she was a fightin & a climbin and came over the top of the gate landin right where I was standin moments ago.

So much for a cow proof gate.

FENCIN TRIVIA

It's harder to fence in
Goats & Hogs than
Cows & Horses

KITTENS

Would you like a kitten, Sir?
"No thanks, I just had lunch."

TIME - MOON BIRDS

The moon birds are hatched on the moon. Hence their name. The two eggs, male & female, hatch every thousand years. The newborn's diet is the moon. They mature quickly, lay two fertile eggs, cover them with moon dust. The parents depart immediately for Mother Earth. The long flight takes 999 years. Upon their arrival at an isolated spot near the Northpole, they enjoy 1 full year of life on Earth. The pair on Earth die happily together moments after their two eggs hatch on the moon. The life cycle of the moon birds is complete and repeats itself once again. By the time the moon is totally eaten by the babies, it will be the same as one day in eternity.

SLOW ELK

Not real bright
　　not real fast
　　　　slow elk

Tempting bait
　　For grizzly, cougar & wolf
　　　　Winchester curable

Slow Elk
　　Fenceable and brandable
　　　　white man's delight

Herdable and controllable
　　most important
　　　　they're saleable

Slow Elk

RATS IN THE NEWS

Rats respond to GLP-1 (glucagon-like peptiside-1). Great news for obese people and anyone desiring to lose a few pounds. GLP-1 is a powerful appetite suppressor that is capable of reducing food intake up to 95% on rats that haven't eaten in 24 hours. GLP-1 makes the rats feel full, not sick. Scientists plan development of a pill for humans to fight obesity, possibly ready for human testing within two years.

More Rats.

The IRS gives new meaning to 800 numbers. Last year the IRS answered 8% of the calls on their 800 toll free question lines.

Youth Smoking Increases.

Some 300 teenagers start smoking every day. Rats. 100 of them will die of smoking related diseases.

Children across the county are organizing protests and letter writing campaigns as student involvement against tobacco increases.

Legal drug dealers! Rats, Beware!

Illegal drugs: opium - Heroin former largest, best known dealer "Khun Sa" has agreed to surrender, other large dealers have come to terms with government officials and will continue with business as usual. Rats!

Miami Smuggling

Cocaine is still #1 in Miami.

Number 2 is a surprise. The street name is "Freon" CFC-12 (chlorofluorocarbons). Selling at $14 per pound.

Illegal drugs for cars.

Rats

FROM A KITTEN TO A CAT

She was young
    eighteen, Jewish
She was beautiful
    long black hair
Short and small
    except 42 D

From Greenich Village
She came to Santa Fe
    and me.

She was a kitten
    young, playful, and tender
One year
    laughin & gigglin
Learnin fast
    meowin & purrin,

Sadness - moving on
    Seattle bound
Two years later
    enroute
Seattle to New York
    Denver Airport
    layover
    12 hours.

Older and wilder
    wonderful
        except
Wounds, blood
    and scars.

My back
    cat clawed.

From a kitten
    to a cat.

CHEE

We didn't want a dog
soft, grey & furry
on our doorstep.

Starving, eating dried
dung, weeds & insects.
We helped his diet
the dullness disappeared.
Alert, energetic & playful
we became attached.

Sleeping under the car
crunching sounds.
Cries of pain
looking bad
Moving slow
in pain
sleeping & eating
looking better
there's hope.
Sometimes a lion
sometimes a bear
sometimes a nuisance.

Part Chow
Part mystery
Part spirit
Chee.

EVEN A DOG'S LOVE IS HARD TO UNDERSTAND

Even a dog's love, is hard, to understand and I ask you, why, he loves you best right after, rollin in, fresh manure or right after, chasin a skunk.

Even a dog's love is hard to understand.

FROG

What a wonderful bird
  the frog are
When he stand
  he sit almost
When he hop
  he fly almost
He ain't got
  no tail hardly either
When he sit
  he sit on what
He ain't got almost
        Anonymous

A GOOD DOG, SPOT

A sitter
  a pointer
    and a
        Sooner
Spot was
  a good dog
Faithful and true
  my protector
    long ago
He was
  a sitter
    and a
        pointer
Sat in front
  of the old ice box
    pointing to
        the meat department
Spot was a good dog
  He was a sooner
    sooner go
        on the floor
          than outside

PRO LIFE

I'm pro life
all life.
too many people
not enough Buffalo.
I'm pro life
all life.
Too many people
not enough Buffalo.
Too many people
not enough Buffalo.

ECOLOGICAL DISHWASHER

Ecological dishwasher
no electricity
no gas
no water
Four legged,
old sheep
big tongue
Dishwasher supreme
Efficient - just whistle
Never breaks down
never complains
Happy tail waggin
old sheep
Ecological dishwasher

SORTIN BEANS

Even the poorest of the poor, sort their beans.

The wild ones are the only ones worth havin.

CATS: TOM AND SELDOM SEEN

On the farm, when I was a boy we had cats, farm cats, some wild, some tame. Hay and grain, mice & rats, cats delight, No poison.

Number one cat, Tom, big & grey, struttin tall, ugly & sweet, tough & tame, milkin time, always waitin, always alert, squirt of milk, expert catcher, old Tom.

In the yard, a nuisance, backin up, rubbin his rear, against my leg tail a switchin, pull me, pull me, by the tail, clawin dirt, tomcat growls, dust cloud, gravel flyin, pull toy alive.

Tom, ears mostly gone, wounds and scars, King cat, Tom cat, only one, miles around, killed the rest. Baby kittens, tom ate 'em, few survived, population control.

Seldom seen, calico cat, mother cat, wild, slinkin low, long & lean, a flash, a shadow, movin fast, seldom seen, never touched, kittens half grown, her's survived, never counted, never touched, seldom seen.

South of the house, cribs of corn, shovels & picks, shellin corn, hard work, 40 cats, hungry & watchin, ready & waitin, mice & rats, escape attempts, feast day.

Timber tunnel for the sheller, finishin a crib, I picked up a timber, mouse nest, baby mice, dozen or so, runnin fast, all directions. A pounce, calico cat, I don't believe my eyes, one in her mouth, one under each foot, 40 cats, no challengers, 5 mice, she took 'em all, fed her kittens, Feast day!

FAST CYCLE

3 seconds
not long
long enough
for a fly
to land
to eat
throw up
eat again
and shit.

3 seconds
not long
long enough.

For a fly.

BUFFALO FACTS

Buffalo killers
Crazy white man
Whisky drinkers
Killers and skinners
Buffalo facts
Of those killed
Only half, were skinned
Of those skinned,
Only half, were picked up
Of those picked up
Only half, were shipped
Of those shipped
Only half, were sold
Of those sold
Only half, were used
Buffalo facts
Crazy white man
Whisky drinkers
Buffalo killers

Buffalo facts

OLD MARE

Horse herd
Uncle Floyd
farmin
with horses
Boss horse
old mare.

Bitin & kickin
maintainin
her position
number one
peckin order
Boss horse
old mare.

Early mornin
bushel of corn
in the stalls
door open
sometimes
on the ground
in front of
the closed door.

Beat on the
empty tin basket
thunderin hoofs
down the lane
Dead run
around the corner
skiddin to a stop

in front of
the closed door
or runnin
to her stall.

Old mare
always in
the lead
first to eat
boss horse.

Pretty ordinary
    except
The old mare
had a defect
a handicap.

No eyes!

HORSE

She was a rather ordinary horse, average in size, common bay color of brown with black mane, tail & black feet. Shaggy with her winter coat. Gentle, strong, dependable, slow but steady. Safe for children & greenhorns, not likely to cause anyone trouble I thought as I saddled her up in mid-afternoon that late fall day. We needed to go up north to bring home the yearling calves. It was overcast, yet warm for late November. I tied a light jacket behind the saddle just in case.

It was a pleasant ride over the rolling hills of grass 6 miles to the north. I easily located the calves in the NE corner of that pasture, rounded them up and headed towards home. It was now late afternoon, the weather was changing, threatening heavy clouds. A gentle breeze, a feeling of closeness and damp-ness prevailed. I put on the jacket, glad I had brought it along.

Within sight of the first gate, we had the calves and were prod-ding the stragglers & wanderers back together when it started to snow lightly with the largest snowflakes I'd ever seen. They were so heavy I could feel them landing on me one at a time. I thought of the old saying "big snowflakes mean big snow" that my father often said. As we neared the tall posts with the open gate it continued to snow heavier and heavier. I thought of the five miles remaining of our journey, hoping it would lighten up and hold off. The calves were getting hard to see with their backs covered with snow. I was barely able to see the stragglers to prod them along with the rest of the herd.

Quickly the snow increased to where I couldn't see the calves, then to a density that I couldn't even see my horses head or ears in front of me. My head felt extra heavy and I realized snow had built up on my hat. As I dumped several inches of heavy snow off, I considered my plight. Five miles from home in a blinding snowstorm with the wind swirling round & round.

I had no idea which way home was. The temperature had dropped enough that my mustache had frozen with the melt-ing snow. I was holding the reins and not controlling the horse's direction, realizing the futility of me choosing where to go, I dropped the reins over the saddle horn. I simply hoped her animal instincts would take us to the barn and home. I had the sensation that the horse was not going in a straight line, that we were often changing direction. Visions of never getting back, dying, being buried under the snow flashed through my mind.

Hours went by, an eternity passed, it seemed like forever. It got darker, obviously the sun had gone down. At least I wasn't feeling any numbness as I wiggled my cold toes & fingers, just cold enough to be uncomfortable I thought. I still couldn't see the horse's head, hadn't seen anything but snow for hours.

I continued to dump the snow off my hat periodically, guessing that 2-3 feet had fallen. All seemed hopeless, I had nearly given up completely when it calmed and I realized we were in the passageway through the windbreak and I could faintly make out the dim outline of trees.

We were home! Feelings of relief, gratitude and joy swept over me. As we neared the barn, protected from the wind I could faintly see objects in front of me. I figured out they were calves. Surprised, I gathered up the reins and rode around them trying to get a count, impossible, I thought as I counted 26 head. I quickly shut the gate and headed for the barn. Dismounting, I opened the door and let the horse to go on into her stall. I followed shut the door, turned on the light, removed the saddle and blankets.

When I went to remove the bridle, I saw that her eyelashes were frozen shut. "Unbelievable, impossible" I said aloud "she can't see a damn thing."

THE HORSE RACES

Granddad Otis said to bet on the "Grey". Uncle Francis said to bet on #1. Mom said to bet on the Jockey and that's why Uncle Francis preferred the dog races. NO Jockeys.

LONG TIME WAITING

We had a team of Belgium mares when I was a boy. Real big, about a ton each. They were very gentle. Belle, the strawberry roan was about like an oversized pet kitten. Dad always kept them in as they were used for all kinds of odd jobs.

We used to go out to the barn on summer days and crawl all over them. It was always cool inside the big barn. Doors open on the north and south made a nice breeze.

I was down beside Belle barefooted when a fly bit her. She picked up a front foot to get rid of it and came down on my foot. It didn't hurt as there was a lot of straw on the floor, but I couldn't get my foot out and couldn't get her to move. I was a long time waiting for another fly to bite her so that she would pick up that foot again.

by my dad Mark Randall

My words are like the stars that don't change.
Seattle

There was a time when I had a choice...
Red Eagle

VAGUE MEMORIES

I remember clearly
a pile of potatoes
west of the corral
horses inside
big ones
too young
to count 'em
too long ago
to picture them
in my mind
vague memories
Belle & Tops
the best team
everyone said
extremely large
even for Belgians
a pair of roans
blue and red
Belle was the red one
birthday same as Dad
When Belle was 35
strong & healthy
choked on a potato
died
Vague memories

THE TEAM

When I was small
we had a team
Buck and Red.

I'd drive'em
thru the gates
from bunk
to bunk
feedin cattle.
Horses, big ones
almost a ton-each
Belgians, beautiful
real horses
workin horses
Buck and Red
Buckskin Mare
Red roan geldin.

My favorite
was Red
bigger, taller
flashier
front legs
oh, so wide
bigger muscles.

I always thought
Red pulled more
than his share.
One cold
winter mornin
snow and ice
trench silo
steep and slick
a heavy load
half way up
Red slipped
stumbled & fell
Buck drug
him and the load
up and out
-alone-.

FANCY BANQUET
SURVIVED & DESCRIBED

My Uncle Carl, big German
    Ran a junkyard, first time around
Ran a ranch, second time around
My mom's sister, Aunt Ethel
    Settlin down, fifth time around
Almost in the sandhills, near Broken bow
    The Log Ranch, between Callaway & Oconto
Cows on the clay hills, corn in the draw
Fancy banquet, uncomfortable rancher
    Didn't quite fit the occasion
        or the suit & tie.
Fancy linen tablecloths, matchin napkins
    clean, white and bright, silver shinin
The food was overcooked, overpriced & cold
    my Uncle Carl said it needed more than
        prayin over.
The straight back chair
    became less than comfortable.
Too many people crowded into too small a pen.
    He was real glad folks had cleaned up some
The very enthusiastic feller told a little joke
    on the speaker, made some big compliments
described all them credentials but couldn't hide
    his fat or this past.
The speaker told a little joke about
    on the way over, then he spoke too long,
        lots of words but very little meanin.
Came home late, indigestion
    Fancy Banquet survived
        never again.

If you want to hear God laugh
tell him your plans.

DESERT DOG

Welcome to the
   Desert Dog
   no barkin
   no growlin
Desert Dog Diner
   Pahrump Nevada
   Frontage road
   Highway 160
Breakfast menu
   Served 6 a.m. to 9 a.m. daily
   Seven specials
   Only 99¢
All American
   Except
   French toast and
   Texas gravy & biscuits
Sorry no substitutes
   Some prostitutes
   Down the road
   Burger Special 99¢ anytime
Sides, soups and salads
   clubs, subs and sandwiches
   Dinners too
   Ham, beef, chicken,
   meat loaf, taco plate
   chicken fried steak
   Texans too
Desert Dog
   100% pure beef
   Vienna hotdogs
   Chicago famous
Desert Dog
   Steak and Seafood
   Ice Cream too

In house specials
Breakfast, lunch
and dinner
Open 7 days
6 a.m. to 9 p.m.
Welcome
to the
Desert Dog
no barkin
no growlin

PAYCHECKS

Why do postal workers get $18 an hour?
When McDonalds workers get $5 an hour?

ON LISTENING

Listen! or your tongue will make you deaf.
Cherokee Saying

These were not our ways. We kept our laws and lived our
religion. We have never been able to understand the white
man, who fools nobody but himself.
Plenty Coups 1848

What can your church do for me,
that God can't do?

SMOKEY, HE AIN'T FOR SALE

My Grandfather Otis had a special horse and his name was Smokey. Grey with lots of white hair and large dark blue-grey to black spots. The fancy black saddle and bridle were well decorated with shiny silver. Being well groomed and shown with this fancy riggin made Smokey look like quite the star, which of course he was, havin been well trained by my Grandfather to do every trick he had ever seen a horse do and more.

They were quite the hit at all the horse shows, parades, celebrations and such around the country. The pair enjoyed showing off all the grand tricks, themselves and all.

My Grandfather had farmed and ranched in his younger days. In more recent times he had bought and sold livestock, mostly hogs, cattle and horses. He was well aware that damn few horses sold as high as a hundred dollars. Well my Grandfather believed everything had a price and people were always wantin to buy this fancy horse and outfit and always askin him how much money it would take to buy him. My Grandfather always said two thousand dollars which meant "he ain't for sale" as no sane person would of paid even five hundred.

Well one Sunday afternoon at a particularly large horse show Smokey's exceptional performance had won them a big purple ribbon and the large crowd had gone wild. After the show my Grandfather and Smokey headed toward the car and trailer and stopped to visit. A small group gathered around commentin on what a beautiful, smart horse he was, and how much they enjoyed the show, and askin the usual questions of how did my Grandfather ever teach a horse to do such and such a trick, how old was Smokey, and so forth. My Grandfather always very patiently answered all the questions as he had never been able to teach Smokey to talk. The well wishers had about run down when this well dressed stranger asked my Grandfather how much would you sell this horse and riggin for?

You all know the answer to that already. What you don't know is that this damn fool dug out $2,000.00 - bought Smokey and the fancy dandy saddle, bridle, blanket and stuff right there on the spot. My Grandfather was of course blinded by all this money, excitement and all. The stranger loaded up Smokey in his new truck and fancy trailer and drove off. My Grandfather headed out in his car and old trailer feelin very rich and lighter as the trailer was empty.

The next week my Grandfather sadly told my Grandmother that he sure wished Smokey wasn't gone, and that he never ever thought anyone would buy him. My Grandfather had sold thousands of horses in his livestock business with nary a regret. Well this was different, and he wasn't prepared to break this special attachment and bonding between him and this ole hoss. My Grandfather was definitely in mournin.

A month later my Grandfather drove the 400 miles to try and buy back this special horse. To make a long story short, two years later after many trips and much hagglin, the new owner who wasn't a stranger any more, felt sorry for my Grandfather and sold Smokey back at a nice profit. He also kept the fancy saddle and riggin. He didn't feel that sorry for my Grandfather.

Everything returned back to normal at the house and barn. He made a new outfit for Smokey in the leather workshop down in the basement. My Grandmother sure was glad Smokey was back home as my Grandfather had been damn hard to live with for the last two years.

It wasn't long till they were back performin, enjoyin life and each other with a fancier outfit than before. After the shows a small group would gather round making comments and asking questions as usual. Whenever someone would ask him "How much would you take for that horse" my Grandfather was always right quick to answer: **Smokey, he ain't for sale.**

REAL MEN

Real men
don't eat
Keesh
and
They don't
eat tou fou
down in
The Bayou.

HAPPY AMERICAN MEN

If you want to be happy
Drive older American cars
Import younger Asian women
Both are easier to maintain.

THE MENU

Hassib's Restaurant
Flagstaff, Arizona
Excellent food.
Hole in the wall
Simple decor
Simple sign,
Todays menu
two choices
Take it
or
Leave it.

WRITERS DINING

Writers dining, on memories,
contemplating words,
down the hatch, for dessert.

FOOD

When it's smokin, it's cookin, When it's black, it's done!
Mom's cookin, pretty bad. Cream of wheat with lumps, yuk!
Actually she fixed somethin really good - pies, apple, rhubarb,
pumpkin - delicious!

I remember when the Bethel county church "Ladies Aid Soci-
ety" did a cookbook to raise money and they asked mom for
her recipes, well she couldn't admit she didn't have any. Mom's
a compulsive liar.

She went thru the farm magazines and hand copied some of
the recipes for the cookbook, representin them as her own.

CHOCOLATE BROCCOLI

Chocolate broccoli
Healthy
almost.
Mentally disturbed
by the
Excretement of life
in hell.
Chocolate broccoli
Healthy
almost.

LIFE

What is life? It is a flash of a firefly in the night... the breath of
a buffalo in the winter time... a little shadow which runs across
the grass and loses itself in the sunset.
Crowfoot 1821

SOUTHERN RASPBERRIES

We flew
　　into New Orleans
　　　　My Dad and I
Rented a car
　　Checked the City
　　　　Headed for the country
Stopped to stretch
　　Walked a bit
　　　　Along a fencerow
Vines and bushes
　　Red berries
　　　　Raspberries
I tried one
　　Delicious
　　　　My Dad tried one
Many raspberries later
　　We both agreed
　　　　Best we'd ever had
Hours later
　　Pickin and eatin
　　　　Walkin and lookin
Big old oak trees
　　moss hangin
　　　　Beauty everywhere
I looked at this
　　Big beautiful
　　　　Red raspberry
　　　　　　and
I noticed on my hand
　　Next to this raspberry
　　　　a tiny red spot
It was barely visible
　　As it slowly moved
　　　　across my hand
Further investigation
　　and observation
　　　　of this beautiful raspberry
Revealed a million
　　Tiny red spots
　　　　all slowly moving
My father
　　was all done
　　　　Eatin
Southern Raspberries

212

HOT DOG

200 brands
300 shapes & sizes
20 billion $'s a year
hot dog
50 million a day
17.5 million pounds
dead meat
recycling potential
233,000 people a day
dead meat

Hot dog

BROWNIES

Real chocolate, extra chocolate
In the oven, smelling good
Buzzes buzzes, door open
hot & done, smelling wonderful.

Can't resist, she cuts the center
I cut the corner.
Tastes great! chocolate
Real chocolate
Extra chocolate
not sweet, tastes great,
1" trail around the edge,
Empty center growin larger.
Going, goin, gone!
Feeling full
chocolate brownies
feelin full,
feelin dull, nap time.

O.D. again
call me, in an hour.

If I can't get up,
Call 911

ROADKILL CAFE

You kill 'em
We grille 'em

Roadkill cafe
Fresh or aged
Naturally tenderized

Your choice
When available
Bruised Buffalo
Thumper on a bumper
Fat cat, sail cat
Collie hit by a trolley
Amtrak Elk
Chunk of Skunk
Sun baked Snake
Smidgen of Pigeon
Swirl of Squirrel
Rigor Mortis Tortise
Slab of Lab
Awesome Possom
Center line Bovine
        and
Today's Special
Cheap Sheep
Poodles & Noodles
        and
For dessert
Road Toad a la mode

Clinton: I didn't ask her to lie on
the disposition, but I did ask her
to lie in a different position.

214

24 HOUR DOUBLE FEAST

Big Black Cow
      Belly deep in grass
            Cow feast
                  All day

Big Black Clouds
      Evening storm
            Wind & rain
                  Thunder & lightnin

Big Black Cow
      Down and dead
            Coyote feast
                  All night

PICKUP

Texas truck
No rust
high miles.

No charge
for extra
dents.

AM FM
stereo cassette
with booster
large radials
only $975.

I'd prefer less people to more jobs.

LARRY'S '38 CHEVROLET

$35.00 - It was a little rough. Cracked fenders, rusted out, bad paint, torn and worn upholstery. Today I realize it was already a junker. Of course being Larry's first car, it was "wonder car."

Lots of hard work, cleaning and fixing. Montgomery Ward's special flow auto paint. Green with black fenders and red wheels. Beautiful.

Larry came by to show off his pride and joy. We hit the dip about 60 MPH for a good bounce. The water came spraying up on us thru the floor. We spent the rest of the afternoon stuffing old socks and rags into the cracks and holes.

Do you remember the ride into Gibbon, becoming airborne on the hilltops, sliding around all the curves, wide open on all the straight aways. Slowly turning the corner on Main Street as the tie rod fell off. It is a miracle any of us are here to remember.

One night we split the manifold. Joel had learned to weld. We were in a hurry to go cruising and show off. The manifold slipped and that is what happened to Larry's front teeth. Time went by quickly, it took a little longer than we expected.

2:30 a.m. We headed out, sounding like low flying aircraft, the exhaust straight out of the manifolds, windows down so we could hear better and get "fresh air." We circled the yards and houses of our friends, wide open in low gear to the delight of us "young" ones and the dismay of sleeping parents. Old Man Bailey was looking for his shotgun as we roared out of sight but not out of sound.

Once we were hunting Jacks to sell for 15¢ each after a big snow when we came upon a dip drifted full of snow. Well, we backed up about a half a mile, wide open, snow flew and when we could see again we were right in the middle of the dip. That night we became tireder and wiser.

Larry eventually got tired of pouring oil and tightening the rods, not to mention the dust and water coming in all the holes. The socks and rags never totally did the job. The '38 ended-up in Dancer's junkyard. Larry had definitely run it down to the last mile. Wrong - I bought it for $15.00 - and after a little work it was off to the races again. But that is another story.

It is good to know, that machoism, is alive and... well. Well... Sick in Nebraska.

DESIRE

A man wants to satisfy desire.
A women wants only to desire.

ASSUMPTION ACCURACY

Assumptions: usually off about 180 degrees.

EXTREME MEASURES

Man is the only land animal that goes to such extremes measures to shit in the water.

People are easily attracted by the superficial.

1959

Lots of chrome
fancy Mercury hardtop
cruising & drinking
fender skirts, continental kit
black & shining.
My friend Lacy
big inheritance
lying & dreaming
Nebraska College
women chasing.
Attorney father
orphaned young
beer drinking
slow Southern drawl
always smiling.
From Louisiana -
Kearney, Ne how? why?
Sweet, smooth & cool
flunking out fast
never knew studying.
Sunday morning
cruising & drinking
3 blondes, Case Hall
parking & talking
I married one.
Cruising & drinking
Lacy's $ gone
over 30 years ago
he left town never to be heard
from again.
Where's Lacy?
I often wonder.

The artless are usually in charge of running the arts.

1955 PLYMOUTH

Monday morning
A blue 1955 Plymouth
in the parking lot.
Keys in the ashtray.
He had the same job for 15 years.
Lived in the same house for 12 years.
Quiet, responsible, never missed a day
or a payment in his life, dependable.
Gone! His landlady couldn't believe it
we couldn't believe it.
The search was on
he owed us $600.00.
Vanished - no one knew where.
Two years later, Las Vegas, Nevada
Skid row.
Wino.
No money - no payments

1955 PLYMOUTH #2

Sun city retirement community.
they were in their 60s, middle
class, nice, clean, well dressed.
They signed for their daughter's
1955 Plymouth. She was soft,
working as a secretary-receptionist.
One month later, ghetto boyfriend,
sex, drugs, abuse - on the skids.
Three months later - she was hard,
scars, unkept in the county jail.
Aging, sad, disappointed parents
making payments on a 1955
wrecked Plymouth, abandoned
in the ghetto.

1955 PLYMOUTH #3

Cotton farm - Buckeye, Arizona 1961. They were cotton pickers, white trash. He was skinny, teeth yellow & missin. Stooped and downtrodden, mumblin with a thick southern accent, while lookin downward. She was heavy, pregnant. A two year old girl clingin & pullin at her torn dress screamin & cryin for somethin to eat. She was ignored.

Returnin form South Carolina the baby died in Mississippi, quickly buried on the roadside. The 1955 Plymouth broke down in Oklahoma and was abandoned.

Back in Arizona livin in a shed, no car, no baby, no money, 3 year old cryin & screamin for food. Authorities prosecuting, child neglect & abuse, improper burial. 1955 Plymouth balance $579.32.

April 12, 1991 - Today I shed my first tear for the dead baby & the hungry, abused little girl.

SANDHILLS DRIVEWAY - SANDHILLS DIRECTIONS

Go 5 miles north of town on the blacktop. Then go 20 miles west on the gravel to our ranch gate. Just follow the main tracks about 30 miles to our place. If you're goin to Jims, just bear west there by our barn and follow the main tracks another 20 miles.

OBEYING

The white man does not obey the Great Spirit, that is why the Indian can't agree with him.
Flying Hawk

BIGGEST HILL IN THE WORLD

Bicycle Hill
Speed memory
A childs world
Around the curve
over the hills
Biggest hill around
See the world
Wood River
Winding & flowing
Gibbon to Kearney
Valley fields
Hills of grass
Beautiful view
Then & now
Back again
Remembering back
Peddlin fast
pegged out
Childhood memory
50 MPH
The biggest hill

BLACK MESA

Black Mesa, singing water
Indian reservation, old Indians
Lacking in, the social skills, of deceit and lies
Living in a, simpler way
Teaching us, to forget, the illusion
Of being, God's gift, to the universe
Indian reservation, old Indians
Singing water, Black Mesa

I know every stream and every wood...
like my fathers before me, I live happily.
Ten Bears

RED, WHITE, NO BLUE

White lights flashing
miniature USA
Eifel Tower
Highway 95, Nevada
Casino, market
Restaurant, bar
Truck stop
Rest stop
Red light beacon
Slowly rotating
Las Vegas's
Closest Brothel
Cherry Patch Ranch
Legal and moral
Open 24 hours
Support your
Local hooker
Coffee cups, T-shirts
And baseball caps
  all
Red and White
 no blue.

THE SPIRIT OF BURMA SHAVE

Lives on in Oklahoma 1997
Four signs properly spaced
Okie Farmers
  Love their land
    Throw your junk
     In the can.

Listen to that deeper need that is
inside you and celebrate filling it.

WELCOME TO LAS VEGAS, NEVADA

It was sundown, gas station pay phone. Short line, 2 women, hookers, working girls, telephone not working, won't take coins. They swear, stroll on.

I look around, no phones in sight. I get out my case, knife that is and poke and pry in the coin slot, retrieving one thin dime, enough for a phone call.

Frustration growing, phone not working. Right hand hammer no results. It was then I spied the button, coin return it said. Of course I pushed it, magic sounds of coins falling and landing. 95 cents, I put in a dime, still not working. Damn, I remember the button and push again $1.55, push again $2.00.

Phone still not working but I'm beginning to see the humor in the situation as I go for the coin return button once again getting $2.55 and a dial tone. One free phone call plus pay telephone jackpot of $6.95.

Welcome to Las Vegas, Nevada.

RUSH & RUSH
MORE & MORE

Rush & Rush to play more & more.
Rush & Rush to learn more & more.
Rush & Rush to work more & more.
Rush & Rush to earn more & more.
Rush & Rush to acquire more & more.
Rush & Rush to take care of more & more.
Rush & Rush More & More
Rush & Rush More & More
Rush - more Rush - more
Rushmore, Rushmore, Rushmore
Mount Rushmore.
Inspired by Mount Rushmore National Park, Black Hills, SD.

NEVADA NUCLEAR

Working at Nevada Nuclear test site, two no more, oil field drilling rig, big one, no oil, big hole, big bomb, big theft, Shoshone land.

Two N's, Nevada & Nuclear.

Test site, big hole, big cable, big cage, two story, two men, two phones. Down the hole, inspection inspected, samples collected, starting back up, falling rock, cage wedged, cage stopped, big machine, big cable, big gauge, 90,000 pounds maximum, shut down.

Stuck, two story cage, two men, two phones, water rising. Basement hot line "God damn it, I'm gonna drown, crank her up and give her hell, pull us out or break something trying."

Big site, big machine, big budget, big bombs, big paychecks, big bureaucracy, big request, to go beyond, the 90,000 pound max. Formal requests, formal recommendations, passed up the chain of command, bureaucratic hot potato, back & forth, here & there.

Two cages, two men, one drowned, water rising. Second day, second story, second man, second telephone, hotline burning, second man, swearing & screaming, demanding, crank her up & give her hell, there's nothing to lose, I'm gonna drown anyway."

Intensified formal requests, formal recommendations, passed up & down, around & around, Bureaucratic hot potato.

No decision, no permission, no action. Second story, second phone, silent now, second man, drowned.

Bureaucratic hot potato, third day, deuces are wild, two dead, two drowned. Big two conference, government & military, big two decision, crank her up, 130,000 pounds max.

Big machine, big cable, big gauge, 120,000 pounds, out it came.

Big bureaucracy, big budget, big bombs, big paychecks, big site big decision, too late, big boo-boo.

Two no more, workin at Nevada Nuclear test site.

IN THE WIND

Women - don't spit into the wind.
Men - don't piss into the wind.

There was a time when our people covered
the land as the waves of a wind-ruffled sea...
that time long since passed... I will not mourn...
Seattle

LIFE

Life is kinda like squeezing laughter from an onion.

GALLUP, NEW MEXICO

Retail at wholesale
50% off, factory direct
largest selection
highest quality
jobber, manufacturer
dealer only
Indian jewelry
Gallup, New Mexico
Route 66, Historic, scenic
Downtown, broken bottles
Tokay wine, broken bottles
broken promises, broken treaties
broken Indians
mostly Navajo, some Hopi
other Indians
from all directions
Tokay Indians
drawn by
The Gallup magnet
warriors of the wine
Tokay scared,
worn and wounded
Beg, borrow & steal
Tokay wine, Tokay Indians
Gallup, New Mexico

LEAVING DENVER

Snow capped mountains
    beautiful, mighty Rockies.
Interstate 70, heading east
    grasslands, flat.
She sez "The Empire State building
    No, it's a grain elevator."
She's from New York
    and I thought, looks like my ex-wife.
They passed the amendment
    land values have skyrocketed.
My cousin informed us.
    Leaving Denver.

ROAD TO RUIN

Highway 54
Corona New Mexico
Old Wade Bar
Now Jessie's Place
Coors Beer sign
Big Cross
Jessie's Place
Big Sign
The Road to Ruin
Highway 54
Duran New Mexico
Duran Dun Went Down
On the road to ruin
Logan New Mexico
Highway 54
Big Bar
Big Sign
Whiskey
The Road to Ruin

When I read in the newspaper that more Vietnam veterans had committed suicide since the war than died in the war, I wrote this piece.

VIETNAM

Many died
more since
suicide.
Dead soldiers
who died
for nothing.
Reality
sadness
grief
war
Death.
Vietnam.

Vietnam inspired this piece.

TOO MANY

Too many years
    race against race
        men against women
            too many wars.
Too many years
    nation against nation
        men against men
            too many wars.
Too many years
    religion against religion
        men against nature
            too many wars.

WE NEED

We need
a little
sanity
over here
over there
everywhere.
We need
a little
sanity
over here
over there
everywhere.
We need
a little
sanity.

Stories only happen to people who can tell them.

CITY VISIT

Long ago

Big city

First time

The old farmer kicked the concrete and said "good place to build a city, the ground's too god damned hard to farm anyway."

NEBRASKA SNOW

Big Snow
Big wind

Snow and
more snow

Big Wind
Big Snow
Big drifts
So high
it was
downhill
To the Rockies

NEBRASKA RAIN

Rollin down the road
Dark clouds rollin
Big wind hit
Started to rain
Turned on the wipers
Rainin harder
Turned 'em on high
Rainin harder
Slowed down
Rainin harder
Stopped
Rainin harder
Lookin out
Rainin so hard
Couldn't see
The other side
Of the Window
Rain enough
To put out
the fires of hell

Tie two birds together. They will not be able to fly,
even tho they now have four wings.
Jalaludin Rumi, Sufi

EASY NEBRASKA WINTERS

Back home in Nebraska
We only get winter
Three times a year
Once in the fall
Once in the winter
Once in the spring
It's sometimes mild
between the cold & blizzards
Sometimes it feels warm
when the sun shines
Sometimes it's above zero
in the daytime
Sometimes the wind
doesn't blow
And there ain't
no winter
in the summer
Extreme heat
Extreme cold
Extreme wind
Nebraskans love it
talkin about it
complainin about it
Watchin & talkin
about the weather
cause they can't change it

FRANKLIN, NEBRASKA

Planks - Plunk and Bunk Motel

SAVED IN NEBRASKA

Long Winter
Snow and
more snow
White and cold
More snow
more cold
more wind
Sanity slipping
and then
Saved by the
Albino Snow
Black and Hot
Albino Snow
Black and Hot
Saved in Nebraska

WARM AND ICY

Nebraska cruise
warm and icy
only in Nebraska
85 degrees warm
75 miles per hour
I-80 cruisin
Enjoyin the scenery
Trees and rivers
cows and corn
Readin the signs
Watchin for ice
Danger they say
Only in Nebraska
Warm and Icy
Nebraska cruise

I want to roam the prairies. There I am free and happy.
Santana

ACCURATE INDIAN SOD BUSTER PERCEPTION

Old Indian, observed,
white settler, plowin
prairie grass
Old Indian, shook his head
and said "wrong side up"

NEBRASKA

The world's largest broom factory was in
Danebrog, Nebraska.
The world's largest river flows thru Nebraska:
The underground Ogallala aquifer.
The world's widest, shallowest river is in Nebraska.
The Platte, a mile wide and an inch deep.
The world's richest town per capita was
Hyannis, Nebraska.
The world's sandhill crane population funnels into a
forty mile stretch on the Platte during migration.
The world's largest cattle transporting company is
in Holdrege, Nebraska.
The world's largest railroad hump yard is in
North Platte, Nebraska.
The world's most scenic state is Nebraska
and there are no mountains to spoil the view.

Tornado Bait -- mobile home parks.

Cold feet are not cool.

BULL DEFINITION

A Bull is a male cow that is roped in Arizona,
rode in U.S. rodeos, fought in Mexico
and shot in Washington D.C.

THREE TYPES OF
NON PAYING RENTERS

Those who wish to pay but can't,
Those who can but won't,
Those who can't and wouldn't if they could.

Stop boasting of intellect and learning;
for here intellect is hampering, and learning is stupidity.
Hakin Jami, Sufi

Dad's mule jumped over the fence,
caught her left rear hoof in the fence.
He found her laying on her back with
I leg sticking up thru the fence,
caught between the top 2 wires.
He cut the top wire & she got up & walked away, unhurt.

SIX WORD HISTORY LESSON

What was, isn't. What is, wasn't.

A baby born today has an 80% chance of being the
victim of a divorce by age 15, and another 80% chance
of their own divorce by age 30.

YOU KNOW YOU'RE IN NEBRASKA WHEN

...it's hot & humid and all the signs say Bridges may be icy.

... you see Go Big Red on everything: hats, shirts, cars, trucks, mailboxes, cash registers, markers, windows, peanuts, caps etc., etc.

... you overhear locals talking about what happened over at the Viadock last night and you learn it's the Interstate overpass.

... every intersection has a church or a bar.

.. everyone calls lunch, dinner and dinner, supper.

... you get off the interstate and the main road has 1 set of tracks and they are down the middle of the road. There's grass growing between the tracks.

... the city welcome sign and the come again sign are on the same post.

... there's an ice storm, snow, rain and dust storm all in the same day.

... the wind stops and it's calm and everyone runs outside to see where the tornadoes are.

... no matter which way the wind blows you can always smell a feedlot.

MORE NEBRASKA INFORMATION

The worlds largest porch swing hangs in Hebron, NE.

An elusive water monster inhabits the water at Walgren near Hay Springs.

Kool-Aid was invented in Hastings, NE. So was Vise-grip the worlds best locking pliers.

Custer county is the sod house capital of the world.

America's first rodeo was in North Platte, NE, by Buffalo Bill Cody.

Arbor Day was started in Nebraska City.

All the Westward trails came thru Nebraska. The Oregon, the Mormon, Pony Express, Lewis & Clark.

Nebraska recently had more one room schools than any other state.

First Wild West Show - July 4, 1883 North Platte, NE. Buffalo Bill Cody's home.

First national log rolling contest at Omaha, September 8, 1898.

First 1000 mile horse race June 13, 1893: Chadron to Chicago 13 days where Buffalo Bills wild west show was on.

First Homestead near Beatrice under the Homestead Act of 1862.

Nebraska is first in ethanol sales in the world.

First fort on Oregon Trail - Fort Kearney

World's largest accident & health insurance company is in Omaha, NE.

Nebraska has the largest concentration of slaughter houses in the world.

Cherry County, NE is larger than the state of Connecticut

NE has 3rd highest high school graduation rate in US.

National Liar's Hall of Fame is in Dannebrog.

The 911 system of emergency communication was developed & first used in NE.

Sioux Indians in Harrison makes the world's largest hamburgers.

The world's only recreation of Stonehenge using Vehicles is near Alliance, NE.

Nebraska has the biggest underground water reserve of any state.

The world's largest elephant fossil came from Lincoln County, NE.

The worlds largest hand planted forest is near Halsey.

Nebraska feedlots have over 2 million cattle on feed, that's a 1/2 million more cattle than people, and that's not counting the cows & bulls that created 'em.

Lots of NE farmers went broke raisin too much hell and not enough corn.

Nebraska ships more farm products by rail than any other state, well over 17 million tons.

The worlds largest shamrock is in O'Neill.

He was a fool before meeting her
she just shined a lite on it.

NEBRASKA COWBOY TRADITION

Nebraska Cowboy
Hills and grass
Cowboy heaven
Romantic image
Different reality
Nebraska Cowboy
It's a hard life
Bein a cowboy
Trouble everywhere
A cowboy can
Resist anything
Except---temptation
Cowboy hell
Full and overflowin
Devil needin help
Cowboy heaven
Mostly empty
Damn few arrivin
Cowboy solution
Simple ritual
Religiously executed
Old cowboy boots
Upended on posts
Eternal purpose
Boot soles
Pointin the way
Cowboy heaven

Speak to everyone in accordance with his understanding.
Sufi

Many fatten themselves in the name of religion.

NEW AGE CHRISTIAN NUDISTS

Turn the other cheek
changed to
bare the other cheek
and much more
Casting off demons & devils
traditions and prudes
casting off garments
skinny dippin hymns
Christian nudist conference
motto adopted
Born again
bare again
Newsletter started
Fig Leaf Forum
Goal achieved
Greater visibility
Casting on
Casting off
new age
Christian nudist
Bare the other cheek
Born again
Bare again
New age Christian nudist.

GREAT GRANDFATHER'S GIFT

One acre of land
for the church.

Accepted conditions:

Don't ever ask me to
set foot inside.
Never ask for another
damn thing as long as
I live.

CLASS OF 56 - 1996

The biggest & the best
Then and now
The class of 56
Gibbon High School
Farm kids, town kids
Mrs Balls and foolishness
Classrooms & study hall
Noon walks downtown
Sneaking candy in the afternoon
When was the war of 1812?
Who's buried in Grants tomb?
What's the square root of pie?
Smith's Drug Store
Cherry cokes & peanut busters
16 tons & I walk the line
Skirts, duals & crusin
Gravel flyin, tires squealin
Camels & Lucky Strikes
Studin and workin
Girls in long skirts
Old car racin
Flirtin with girls
Smokin and drinkin
Flirtin with death
Girls in cliques
Giggles and wiggles
Boys doin dirty tricks
Knock, Knock, who's there?
Kilroy, Kilroy who?
Kill Roy Cousins*
Burma Shave
Dates and drive inns
Dairy Queen, A & W
Boys - Voc Ag!
Girls - Home ec.
There's been some changes
12 hour wonders
Responsible teenagers
Doin adult jobs
Hormones workin
Some shy and reserved
Some wild and crazy
240

Rites of passage
Something lost
Something gained
Children to adults
Marriage and divorce
Success and failure
Movin too fast
This class of 56
They said "we couldn't last"

Some won
Some lost
All here but one

It's been quite a ride
We look in the mirror
Same thing only different

Biggest & the best
Then & now
The Class of 56

* Town marshal

1992

March 1992
presidential proclamation
officially declaring
1992
the year of the

American Indian

already drowned
in the hoorah
celebrating 500 years
of Columbus
and Genocide.

1992

This is a rewrite that my ex, Mary Rose and I did. We each rewrote it individually and then we put the two together. The Lord's Prayer rewritten, renamed Spirit Prayer.

SPIRIT PRAYER

Great Spirits who are everywhere,
sacred be all of creation. Your lessons
come, your light be shown to us as it is
in nature. Give us this day strength, love
& guidance to do our service. Teach us
to face fear, that we may learn to love,
share & respect all life. Lead us to blessings
& deliver us in love. Yours is the
power and the mystery & the wonder
forever and ever.

SPIRITUAL SEED

Planted before I was conceived
Sprouted when I was three
Just wanted to be free

Mowed, hailed and stomped on
Life was hard, growin like a weed
Spiritual seed, spiritual need

Just wanted to be free
Youthful energy, spiritual seed
Nearly forgotten, Wild & crazy

Adult failures, crash & burn
dormant seed, Indian watered
Spiritual growth conceived

Planted before I was conceived
Just wanted to be free
Spiritual seed, spiritual need

242

HOT WIRE

Gonna
Hot wire
this reality

One wire
into Mother Earth
One wire
into Father Sky
One wire
into society
Connect them
into Spirituality
Gonna
Hot wire
this reality

CAUTION CHURCH

It has been determined
by the attorney general
that
Religion can be harmful
to your health

Warning signs
must be
displayed

Caution Church

WHAT MAN REALLY KNOWS

Men suppose, fancifully, that they know truth
and divine perception. In fact, they know nothing.
Juzjani, Sufi

1950's

Remembering the 50's
a heavy time
much lighter
than before
or since

Remembering
The music too

In my 50's
Remembering
Reflecting on
The great adventure
of life.

Having lived enough
to know
pain and joy.

Food for the soul
Remembering the 50's
That time
gone forever
Except
in my mind.

Remembering the 50's.

PROTEIN

1 Pound of grasshoppers = 3 pounds of beef

One third of Americans are
unable to snap their fingers.

AFTER CHURCH POEMS

Gene, Gene built
    a machine
the greatest machine
    you've ever seen
Art, Art let a fart
    and blew the whole
damn thing apart!
    compliments of George

Little Willie with a
    thirst for Gore
nailed his sister to the door
    mother cried with humor quaint
Willie dear, don't
    spoil the paint.

compliments of Gitch

CHRISTIAN ATHEIST ANSWER

I asked the Christian,
    where did God come from?
The Christian answered,
    He has always been here.
I chuckled, remembering
    asking my atheist father
Where did the Earth & everything
    come from?
He answered, everything has
    always been here.

He was a believer in disbelief.

RELIGIOUS SHIT

Taoism: Shit happens
Hinduism: This shit happened before.
Buddhism: It is only an illusion of shit happening.
Zen: What is the sound of shit happening?
Islam: If shit happens it is the will of Allah.
Jehovah's Witness: Knock, Knock, Shit happens.
Atheism: There is no such thing as shit.
Agnosticism: Maybe shit happens and maybe it doesn't.
Protestantism: Shit won't happen if I work harder.
Catholicism: If shit happens, I deserve it.
Rastafarism: Smoke that shit.
Televangelism: Send money or shit will happen to you.
Judaism: Why does shit, always happen, to me?
Confucianisn: Confucius say Shit Happens.

HORSE SHOW

Horses' asses
showing
Horses' asses
to
Horses' asses

Sorrow swims and grows big & fat in alcohol.

There is no love like that of most mothers.

Time is the great equalizer

CHOICES

Truth or Illusion
choose one, lose one

The wise, the foolish
the sun shines equally on both.

Real education & learning come from
studying that which we love.

In 1924 the Mescalero Apaches
became citizens of the U.S., at least on paper.

I heard the mocking bird singing in the moonlight.
I knew, that moment, that I would get well.
Lone Wolf

Don't let fear steal your joy.

Humility is reminding self that we are no one
when others think we are somebody.

In life it's better to move & bend than to break
from the wind of hard knocks.

Special: Any two ten dollar items for only $25.

Already made friends with death
Still working on life.

WINDY FRIEND

Windy Friend: Blows & goes,
means well, but tests everyones patience,
like the Nebraska wind.

ARGUING

Why do you want to be the
other half of an argument?

ATTITUDE

Change your attitude
and the world changes.

WHY?

Why do you take by force
what you could obtain by love?
Powhatan

BLINDED

Blinded by hype & lies, most have been living in illusions
so long that the real world and truth are deeply buried.
Happy diggin

TRUTH

How can you miss the water
till the well runs dry?

YOUNG/OLD

Too young to be old
too old to be young.

GETTIN THERE

Point yourself and take one step
then another, and another.

STATISTICS

Statistics are like bikinis;
What they reveal is interesting, what they conceal is vital.

POWER

We have much power we have never used.

LEARNING

You can't learn anything any younger.

REACTIONS

When a normal person has a flat tire,
they call triple A.
When an alcoholic has a flat tire,
they call the suicide hotline.

PEOPLE

Nice people suck, mean people bite.

PEACE

It's hard to shake hands with an angry fist.

ARGUING

Argue with a fool and become one.

SEATTLE

Day and nite cannot dewell together.
Seattle

SYMPTOMS

Symptoms are not the problem, but they point towards it.

MISTAKES

Farmer and Ranchers take responsibility for their big
expensive mistakes, but they often blame their
foolish ones on their wives.

PAST/FUTURE

Do not regret the past and
do not worry about the future.
Dhun-nun (Sufi)

TRUST

Never trust one who cheats at playing solitaire.

NEVADA

You can't beat the climate in Nevada,
you can't beat the slots either.

LAS VEGAS

Our neighbor flew his own airplane to
Las Vegas to get away from it all.
They got it all away from him -
including his plane.

MISTAKES

Mistakes don't pay, the exception is alimony
where a woman makes money from her mistake.

MISTAKES

Attorneys get paid for mistakes and
doctors bury theirs.

MUGGY

A muggy day is when everything that's suppose to stick
together comes apart and everything that's suppose
to come apart sticks together.

PEACE

May the peace of God which passes all understanding,
be with you now and always.

ALLEGIANCE

Remember: Politician's allegiance is only to politics.

COMPARISON

Compare 25,000 years use by native Americans
to 500 years by Europeans.

RIGHTS

We all got the right to be wrong.

FACE WRINKLE TREATMENT

Preparation H is being used to treat face wrinkles quite suc-
cessfully. Negative side effects: can make you look like an ass.

CHRISTIANS

Christians - most hateful, ruthless group of people on the face
of the Earth. Wherever there are white people, there is Chris-
tianity and there are missionaries. They send the Christian
missionaries in first to preach turn-the-other-check, then they
come with their armies to conquer the people.
Nathan McCall

LONGEVITY

If you desire a long life,
avoid dying by practicing healthy living.

NATURE

Nature would be better off if people quite playing God.

POLITICIANS

Politicians are like children playing with matches -
can't comprehend the damage they may cause.

JAPANESE INVESTMENTS

Japanese investments circle this world today
and may capture the world tomorrow.

NEWS FLASH

News Flash: the UN passed a law, beginning in the year
2000 all calendars must be metric.

FREEDOM

The only freedom too many believe in is
"Freedom from personal responsibility."

ROAD TO DRUGS

The road to the drug world is paved with alcohol.

SLEEPING WITH DOGS

If you sleep with dogs, you're gonna get fleas.

REAL COWBOY

Three cowboys in a pickup, which one is the real cowboy?
The one on the left is a truck driver. The one on the right is a
gate opener. The one in the middle is a "real cowboy" as he
does nothin.

REAL FARMER

You might be a real farmer if you've never bought a cap.

PROBLEMS

Most of the problems today wouldn't exist if
those Europeans had come to learn & change
instead of to conquer & convect.

GROWING

Growing always comes with growing pains.

ILLEGAL DRUGS

People doin illegal drugs don't
make me breathe their smoke.

SINNERS

The worst sinners make the best saints.

STRUGGLE

Olive Oatman was captured by Apaches and
recaptured by anglos years later. Her desperate
struggle to get back to her Indian husband and children
shook many peoples belief in civilization.

FOOD ADVICE

Eat cheap food because
the products you excrete are of low value.

NO, I AIN'T DEAF

The motel manager just called to ask me to turn down
the TV cause them folks next door got overly sensitive ears.

OVERSTRESS

Overstress, and then, regress and that's the way it is.

POETIC FACT

Poets making points, have to use a fact now & then.

PICTURE TAKIN ADVICE

When things are goin to Hell,
don't stop to take pictures.

CHEAP

He was so cheap that he squeezed the Buffalo on a nickel
till it shit a dime, then bitched cause it wasn't a quarter.

SWIMMING

A Beaver can hold its breath for 15 minutes
and swim underwater for half a mile!

THE LAW

The law is merely an instrument to
sanctify the crimes of the powerful
and to suppress the aspirations of the less privileged.
Michael Andrews

ROAD MAP

Lots of alcohol and/or drugs will turn
your skin into a road map to Hell.

TOBACCO & MILK

Tobacco is not addictive but
too much milk might be bad for us.
1996 presidential candidate Dole

LOVE & HATE

When love swells, hate shrinks.

PERSEVERANCE VS INTELLIGENCE

Perseverance will overcome intelligence every time,
and I'm going to stick to it.
Alabama Representative Don Young

MESSIAHS

Live messiahs are dangerous to the established order
and are killed in the name of god & country.

POTENTIAL GREAT POET

Could'a been great if it wasn't for
too much money, education & prestige.

LOVE

Love don't knock when it comes.

SMART, SMARTER, SMARTEST

Smart - Knows it's all B.S.,
Smarter - Accepts it all anyhow,
Smartest - Loves it all anyhow.

CHRIST

Jesus Christ was not a Christian.

30 YEARS OF HOLLYWOOD PROGRESS

Today there are more Hollywood gun owners
in the closet than homosexuals.

HOLLYWOOD EMPLOYMENT

Drug addicts are promoted, conservatives are fired.

OPTIMISTIC HOPE FOR THE FUTURE

Prayin that no one shows up for the next war.

FINAL BIRTHDAY GIFT

After death you don't have any more birthdays.

SICK

Been lickin out the pan of misery too long.

LUXURY

Anyone can afford expensive dreams.

LADDER ADVICE FOR
THOSE AFRAID OF HEIGHTS

Always use ladders in the horizontal position.
Never use a ladder in the vertical position.

EX'S HATED

Ex's hated their ex's usually because,
they knew too much about them.

* * * * * * * * * * * * *

No book would be complete without
a helpful household hint.

Here it is:
HELPFUL HOUSEHOLD HINT

Need a strainer?
Can't find one?
Use the fly swatter.

JOEL RANDALL
WRITER: ESSAYS & POEMS of the Heartland - programs available.
COLLECTOR: TRUCKS, PICKUPS & CARS 1935-1965
P. O. Box 1712 - Kearney, NE 68848 - (308) 468-5266

Order Form

Books

REFLECTION & PERCEPTIONS
    by Joel Randall   ____ @ $14.95 each   ____

COWBOY OR FARMER?
    by Joel Randall   ____ @ $9.95 each   ____

ESSENCE
    by Joel Randall   ____ @ $9.95 each   ____

Audio Cassette Tapes

FARM AND RANCH MEMORIES
    by Joel Randall   ____ @ $7.00 each   ____

Shipping & Handling $3.00   ____

Total Enclosed   ____

Please send your order to:
Joel Randall
Heartland Publishing
P.O. Box 1712
Kearney, NE 68848
(308) 468-5266

Entertaining programs are available for any occasion.

TEAR OUT
THIS PAGE
AND
ORDER THAT GIFT
FOR
SOMEONE SPECIAL.

INDEX

ABOUT THE AUTHOR
Joel Randall 1939-?

Grew up northwest of Gibbon, Nebraska with crops and livestock. Attended a one room school, graduated from college in Kearney, corporate educated - Arizona.

Part of a "Summerhill" type school in New Mexico. Built a place, trained horses, milked goats, fed the hogs. Established a plumbing business. Developed an alternative healing center. Owned and operated a motel and mobile home business, moved back to Nebraska where I write while enjoying the old vehicle hobby and family life on the farm and ranch.

Published: Auto Clubs & Writers Groups Newsletters, This Old Truck, Dry Crib Review, Twelve Steps Times, Mile High Poetry Society Anthology "Helicon", Santa Fe Sun, Santa Fe Reporter, Man Alive, Mother Earth News, Self published books and audio cassettes.

Readings & Programs: Schools, Retirement facilities, Coffee houses, Cowboy poetry gatherings, Literature festivals, Various celebrations and events in Arizona, Colorado, Nebraska, Nevada, New Mexico, Kansas and Texas.

My Father Mark Randall
1915-1995

A lifetime of farming and ranching. From horses and the depression to air conditioned cabs and chemicals. He knew the prairie and six generations on the same place, groomed my two sons to carry on.